Real Estate and Tax Deed Investing

W9-BYJ-473

Real Estate and Tax Deed Investing

How We Made Over One Million Dollars in Two Years

Matt Merdian and Laurence Samuels

2007

Download your free Tax Deed Sales Location List Now:
www.taxdeedbook.com/download
Code: freedownload

Published by London Meridian Publishing LLC

Printed in the United States of America.

London Meridian Publishing Books are available at a special quantity discount to use for sales promotions, employee premiums, or educational purposes. Please call our sales department at 860-469-2665 to order or for more information or email at info@taxdeedbook.com.

Real Estate and Tax Deed Investing

Contents

Introduction

W elcome to our world. Our names are Matt Merdian and Laurence Samuels, and we are glad you decided to purchase our book. Welcome to your first step towards understanding, and, most importantly, applying the techniques for purchasing Tax Deed properties. We hope our book sends you on your way to achieving financial freedom!

This book was written with everyone in mind.

Are you someone (like us) who hates working a 9 to 5 job with little reward? Are you someone who wants to increase your net worth so you can be secure in your retirement years? Are you someone who wants to be a full time real estate investor? We hate to use the words **FINANCIAL AND PERSONAL FREEDOM** because it is so clichéd, but a career in real estate really can offer you these two important life-changing things. Would you enjoy some extra money to take a vacation with your family? Maybe you have your eye on a new car or a new set of golf clubs? <u>You can execute one well-planned real estate deal per year and provide yourself with ample extra money to do all the things you want</u>. Whether you are researching the possibility of adding real estate investing to your career goals or you are a seasoned investor with hundreds of properties under your belt, this book can benefit you in many ways. We hope you enjoy reading it as much as we enjoyed writing it.

How are we qualified to write this book?

Great question! We founded London Meridian LLC. in May 2003 and have been investing in Tax Deed properties ever since. We are the sole authors of our book and the sole owners of our company. Our book is candidly written about our experiences in Tax Deed investing. By divulging all of our financial successes, we have provided you an honest look into real estate investing.

Our very first Tax Deed property netted us around $45,000 profit with zero remodeling and zero headaches. Yes, $45,000 in 8 months with very little work involved. We even received rental income on the property. Our book provides the EXACT numbers involved in this transaction so you can see how much it REALLY costs to make a real estate transaction of this kind. We think that you'll agree $45,000 is a handsome and very achievable profit!

When writing this book, we used real life examples that we experienced first hand. You will be reading recent real life examples that occurred in the time interval from 2002 to 2007, rather than outdated material and exaggerated results. These results and examples come from our company's actual sales. If you take the time to read this material, you will have a solid understanding of the process of Tax Deed Sales. More importantly, you will then have a <u>very</u> realistic outlook regarding potential returns on your Tax Deed investments.

Why are we writing this book?

Again, this is another great question! Tax Deeds are not a secret or a myth. Misunderstood? We think so. Risky? Yes, they can be; but then again, so is purchasing stocks without researching the stock market! Like any investment, if you are well informed (that's where we come in) and perform your due diligence, you can minimize your risk. Our goal is to tear down the misconceptions of Tax Deeds and give you the real deal on how they work and how you can benefit from these sales. If you understand and apply what you have learned, we know you will be as successful as we have been.

What can you expect from this book?

Honesty, Truth, Facts, Details, Guidance, Direction, and Real Life Examples are what you will find in these pages. Too many real estate books and seminars provide the reader and attendees with hype and unrealistic results. <u>This is not one of those books</u>. We have read over 50 books on real estate and found only a handful to be helpful. Have you ever watched real estate infomercials touting the term "no money down"? Makes you wonder, doesn't it? How can I purchase properties with no money down? The truth of the matter is that most of the time, you can't. This book explains all and gives you a <u>realistic</u> view of how to purchase real estate. Our company was founded on realistic expectations, and realistic expectations are what we want to provide you in this book.

As a prequel, we will first to tell you about the positives of Tax Deed investing, and how to overcome the negatives of Tax Deed investing:

Positives:

- It is easy to learn—anyone can do it!
- There is money to be made in any state that holds Tax Deed Sales.
- Tax deeds offer the ability to purchase various types of property including commercial, residential, and raw land at severely discounted prices.
- With technology and the internet, research is MUCH easier than in prior years.
- Research and persistence makes the difference between unsuccessful auction bidder and constant buying.
- For those willing to take some risks, the reward may be great.
- Find a level of satisfaction of helping out people who are in financial difficulties, while raising neighborhood and home values.
- Potential passive income.
- You could build new relationships with other investors.
- Acquire a new level of awareness of the real estate market that you are investing in.

Negatives; or, as we like to call it, Items to overcome:

- It requires dedication and persistence.
- Research can be time consuming.
- Do not expect to pay for any of these properties 'no money down'.
- You must have some expendable finances. (Don't worry, we can show you how!)
- You must pay for properties with cash in a relatively short timeframe.
- Liability of payments on 'hard money loans'.
- Many people face internal fears of beginning a new business adventure.

Some of these items on the negative list we offer advice and help on. Some of them we cannot. We cannot force you to be dedicated and persistent, and we certainly cannot provide you extra time to research properties. Unfortunately, you are on your own there. What we intend to do is to provide you with all the information you need to make educated decisions and to understand the Tax Deed process. It will be entirely on you as a person to apply everything you learn from us in order to become a successful Tax Deed investor.

CHAPTER 1

In this chapter, you will learn:

- How the Tax Deed process works
- The difference between Tax Deeds and Tax Liens
- How to locate Tax Deed sales
- How to locate and read Tax Deed files

THE TAX DEED PROCESS

A simplified explanation of the Tax Deed process is:

1. People must pay annual county taxes on real estate.
2. If the person or entity does not pay the real estate tax owed, the government auctions the amount owed in return for an interest rate. This is called a TAX LIEN.
3. After a designated time period (generally 2 years), the purchaser of the tax lien can file for a TAX DEED, which forces the sale of the property at a government auction.

This is where WE buy the property...at the TAX DEED AUCTION.

Let's look at this now in greater detail.

HOW IT ALL WORKS:

Every year, property taxes are due. Whether someone owns a house, condo, boat slip, parking space, commercial property, or vacant land, they must pay real estate taxes.

The date the real estate taxes are due differs from state to state. In some states the property owner can make quarterly payments to ease the financial burden. We will use our home county, Orange County in Florida, as an example. The real estate taxes are due on or before March 31st each year.

Most mortgage payments have *escrow* built into the payments.

Escrow is an account held by the mortgage company where funds are paid into the account to cover such items as property tax and homeowners insurance. The bank calculates the escrow amount each year, and then pays out those expenses from the account as needed.

There may be other items held in escrow such as homeowners' association fees, boat slip fees, mortgage insurance, and anything that is a scheduled recurring payment. This escrow is to help ease the burden of providing large lump sums of money when the bills are due. Essentially, it forces the property owner to save money to ensure the bills are paid. There are many people who believe they are disciplined enough to save money and pay the bills when they are due, and therefore do not use escrow. Others who are less self-disciplined use the escrow system to ENSURE their important bills are paid on time.

Throughout this book, we will be using both examples and case studies. Examples are fictitious, while case studies are real life instances. Within these case studies, we have changed the names of the subjects to protect their privacy. Our own identities are the only ones left unchanged.

Example

John has purchased a home for $200,000. His mortgage rate is 5%, interest only. Interest only means John's minimum payment does not reduce the principle amount on his mortgage; only the interest is paid each month. This calculation is easy. $200,000 multiplied by 5% interest annually equals $10,000. This is the annual amount John must pay in interest. Divide by 12 months and that equals $833.33 per month. John has an escrow account with the finance company which is used to pay his real estate taxes of $3600.00 per year. Divide by 12 months again, and that equals $300 per month. This means John pays $300.00 per month for escrow on top of the $833.33 for interest for a total payment of $1,133.33 per month. When due, John's mortgage company will send his tax payment of $3600 to the County. John does not have to worry about paying $3600.00 when it is due because he has been paying money into his escrow account held by his mortgage company. The bank is happy to provide John with this service because it assures them his real estate taxes will be paid, therefore preventing his property from being auctioned at a Tax Lien or Tax Deed sale.

Local Counties needs property taxes from property owners in order to pay for street lights, fire departments, schools, roads, etc. If the property owner does not pay the county the amount that is due, the county will SELL the TAXES in order to collect the owed money! That's right; the county sells the owed tax amount in what is called a **Tax Lien Sale**. Many people confuse Tax Liens and Tax Deeds.

To clarify: Tax Liens are notes held by the winning bidder for a property owner's real estate taxes. The person who holds the Tax Lien note does <u>not</u> own the property, but rather a note or lien for the taxes which are owed.

Tax Liens

Definition:
1. A claim imposed by the federal government to liquidate a person's property so that the owed taxes and other fees can be paid in full.
2. A type of lien placed on a property title when the owner has not paid property, assessment, or other state and federal taxes.

For our purposes, we will use the second definition. At the Tax Lien auction, the government is SELLING the Tax Lien. People will bid against each other for the privilege of paying off the taxes. Bids are made in the form of an interest rate, starting at approximately 18%. As the bidding continues, the bids decrease until the person who is willing to accept the lowest interest rate wins. The winning bidder then holds a lien on the property for the taxes he paid off, and the current owner of the property now owes the winning bidder the owed tax amount PLUS the interest stated on that tax lien.

It may seem odd that the bids go from highest to lowest, but it is logical. In Orange County, Florida, the interest rate begins at 18% and goes down from there. The bidder willing to receive the LEAST AMOUNT of interest on their money will be the winner. The bid goes from highest to lowest because the bidders are bidding against each other in order to determine who will accept the lowest interest return on their money. This is also the government's attempt to try and obtain the lowest possible interest rate for the person in default of their property taxes.

Still confused about Tax Liens? Think of it the following way: When a bank or a mortgage company writes a loan on your property, they place a lien on your property. The mortgage company doesn't own your property at this point, they just own the note backed by a mortgage. If you don't make your mortgage payments, the bank can apply for foreclosure and thus acquire the deed and ownership of your property. Tax Liens work the same way.

Remember, the winning bidder on a TAX LIEN does not receive ownership of the property. All they have done is paid the

overdue taxes in exchange for an interest rate on the owed tax amount.

When the bidder has paid the tax lien amount in full, the county immediately receives their past due taxes. After a set period of time, the exact length of which depends on your state (likely around 2 years), if the owner of the property still has not paid the person that purchased the tax lien in full, then the tax lien holder may apply for a Tax Deed.

This application for a Tax Deed begins the process in which the county offers the property for auction to the general public. If no one bids on the property, it will be "struck to applicant", which means that the person who purchased the tax lien acquires the property.

This process forces the county to sell the property at auction. The tax lien holder, like any other investor, is able to bid on the property to try to acquire ownership. In the very rare case no one bids on the property, the tax lien holder would receive the title to the property. This rarely happens because there are investors (like you) who will attend the auction and attempt to purchase the Tax Deed.

If someone does purchase the property at the sale, then when the winning bidder pays their bid amount, the tax lien holder gets paid the full amount of the original investment plus the additional interest listed on the tax lien.

In Florida, a Tax Lien holder may keep the lien for as long as 7 years before they lose their right to file for a Tax Deed.

Case Study

Jack had been attending the annual Orange County, Florida Tax Lien sale for 3 years, but had never been able to acquire Tax Liens for more than 4% interest. Jack was nearing retirement, and used Tax Liens as secure investments he knew would provide him with guaranteed rates of returns. He also knew there was a possibility that he may be able to acquire the properties he held the Tax Liens on at a later date. Jack always applied for the Tax Deeds after 2 years, since the interest rates were not very favorable. In 2003, Jack attended the Tax Lien sale as usual, but that year he was fortunate enough to acquire several Liens at interest rates ranging from 13% to 16%. After 2 years of non-payment from the owners of the properties, instead of applying for Tax Deeds, Jack decided to keep the Liens for longer periods of times, because the interest rates were so high. The last time we corresponded with Jack, he informed us that he planned to keep these Tax Liens until 2008. He would then apply for a tax deed, hoping to gain ownership of the properties. It is likely that when he applies for the Tax Deed and forces the auction, other people will be bidding for the property. When the winning bidder pays their bid amount, Jack gets paid his original investment plus the additional interest that is owed to him.

Now that you have a general idea of how the process works, let's discuss the elements that will be important in acquiring your first Tax Deed property!

To reiterate our interpretation of Tax Liens: People owe taxes on all real estate, and the government has the right to collect those taxes. If the owner does not pay that tax by a deadline, the government has the power to auction that tax amount to the lowest-bidding individual or entity, in exchange for tacking on an interest rate which the owner of the property must pay in addition to the original tax amount. If this process takes place, the investor has a 'Tax Lien' against the owner's property. Generally, there is a time frame the investor is required to hold the tax lien before he or she is able to force a sale. In Florida, that time is 2 years. The minimum bid will be for the amount owed, plus interest, plus accrued fees for advertising, notice, etc.

Example

Every year, Judy attends the Orange County, Florida Tax Lien sale. This sale is only held once a year, and contains thousands of Tax Liens which are offered for sale by the County in order to collect past due real estate taxes. During the bid process, Judy hopes to be the bidder with the highest interest rate on her bids. During this sale, the bid on each property starts at an 18%. This is the interest rate that will be paid to the winning bidder on top of the real estate taxes which are owed. It is not unusual for Judy to be bidding against large multi-billion dollar companies such as Merrill Lynch. These large companies view Tax Liens as a safe investment. Judy understands that the more valuable the property, the lower the bidders are willing to go on the interest rate. Sometimes she sees interest rates bid as low as 1%. Why would people be willing to receive 1% interest on a Tax Lien? In the hope that at the end of the 2 year holding period, nobody will bid on the property at the Tax Deed sale and would therefore be "Struck to the Applicant", meaning that the person who holds the Tax Lien automatically receives the property without any additional financial outlay. This rarely happens. In fact, we have never seen a "valuable property" be struck to the applicant.

This year, Judy purchases a $5000.00 Tax Lien at 5% interest. This means that Judy has to pay the $5000.00 plus fees. The owner will receive notice that they owe the $5000.00 plus accruing interest of 5%. If the owner pays the $5000.00 plus interest and fees, the lien is satisfied and the property is no longer at risk. If the owner does not pay the $5000.00 plus interest and fees, Judy may file for a Tax Deed after a minimum period of 2 years. This will begin the process to force the sale of property to recover the Tax lien holder's money. The auction where the Tax Liens are sold generally occurs in May. Contact the Tax Collector's Department in the counties you are interested in attending for specific dates. This book does not go into great detail about the process of Tax Liens because our focus is not Tax Lien investing. There are plenty of books out there in the market that cater to Tax Liens. Our focus will be when the holder of the Tax Lien forces the sale and the property then becomes a TAX DEED.

Now that you have an understanding of Tax Liens, let's take a look at our main focus, Tax Deeds!

Tax Deeds

Definition:
A deed on a property issued to the purchaser when the property is sold at a public sale for nonpayment of real estate taxes.

A Tax Deed's definition is relatively simple. The deed on a property is issued after a winning bidder has paid all of the owed real estate taxes and county fees in addition to the bid amount.

In the rare case no one bids on the property for at least the "opening amount" or "opening bid", the property is "struck to the applicant". This means the person or entity who purchased the Tax Lien will now receive a Tax Deed showing ownership of the property.

The auctions we attend in Florida require the winning bidder to provide a **$200 cash deposit** for each property. If you cannot provide the $200 deposit after being declared the auction winner, the property is re-auctioned immediately. Always make sure you come prepared with enough cash to make these deposits when attending an auction.

When a bidder wins the property, the bidder has 24 hours to pay the balance in certified funds, usually cash or a <u>cashier's</u> check. The County office will usually NOT take a personal or business check because it is not certified funds. We recommend a cashier's check or bank certified check. The original owner of the property can still pay off the owed tax amount until the time the new deed is recorded.

We have seen times where the winning bidder did not return with final payment quickly enough; therefore allowing the original property owner to pay off the owed taxes, even though the auction had ended. In these cases, the original owner retains his property by paying the back due taxes and fees associated with the tax deed process, and the winning bidder's $200 deposit is returned by the County.

Case Study

One inexperienced Tax Deed investor named Dennis was lucky enough to be the winning bidder on a 3 bed / 2 bath condo. He was extremely excited about winning his first auction, and his goals included leaving his current 9 to 5 desk job and becoming a full time real estate investor. Unfortunately, after posting his $200 deposit, Dennis ran into some trouble accessing the funds to pay off the total bid amount. Dennis eventually acquired the funds, and returned to the tax office at 9:30 the following morning to make the final payment.

Unfortunately, Dennis was too late. Earlier that morning, the original owner had paid off the owed back taxes before the bidder returned with the funds. Dennis did not receive ownership of the property. Even though his deposit money was refunded, he was bitterly disappointed.

For this reason, when we are the winning bidders, we rush to the bank to obtain the funds we need to close the transaction.

"Redeemed" and "Struck to Applicant"

There are situations when the owner pays off the taxes and fees before or during the sale. This is referred to as being "redeemed". Most of the properties are redeemed for many reasons. The owner may have obtained the funds needed to pay off the debt, or perhaps an investor approached the owner and worked out an agreement to pay off the taxes in return for the owner selling the property at a discounted rate.

A property being "struck to the applicant" is very rare. This usually occurs when the property has little value, or the minimum bid is higher than the market value of the property. For example, desert, wasteland, swampland, an oddly-shaped parcel, landlocked or inaccessible parcels, water-locked parcels, etc. We have seen this happen on many pieces of swamp land in Florida. Remember that many savvy investors watch these auctions, so if a property has value, someone will bid on it.

We are sure there will be plenty of people who will argue the point we have just made. They will say, "It is land, so it must be worth SOMETHING". We understand that almost all land is worth something. That said, however, there will be times when the minimum bid is greater than the value of the property. We see this case with mobile homes and with swamp land. Those pieces of land and property do have a value, but sometimes the value does not exceed the minimum bid, so it is "struck to the applicant".

Case Study

In Volusia County, Florida, there are large quantities of swamp land. Why would anyone want to purchase swamp land? That is a great question. There are actually several sound reasons. Some people may want a piece of swamp property because the state may be attempting to purchase land in the area to keep as designated wetlands. Some bidders may know that surrounding owners are willing to pay a certain amount for the land. Others may own a swamp buggy and need some land to speed around on. The reason people purchase properties that others view as unusable varies case by case. The saying, "One man's trash is another man's treasure," fits well here.

Where do I find Tax Deed Sales?

The Office of the Comptroller is the department that handles Tax Deeds in your county. Our website, www.taxdeedbook.com, has a list of most counties in the United States, along with information about where and when Tax Deed sales take place.

For your local area, we recommend one of 4 ways to locate the sales, in this order:

1   Check the website, www.taxdeedbook.com.

2   At www.google.com, type in your county name, state, and the words "Tax Deed"—for instance, type "Orange County Florida Tax Deed".

3   Call directory assistance and ask for your county's Office of the Comptroller number.

4   Look in your local paper for Tax Deed listings.

www.taxdeedbook.com is simple to use and easy to navigate. Once inside the site, you will have access to approximately 3000 counties. Please visit the site for further details.

We personally used Google to search for our information when we first started. Though there are many search engines available, we believe that Google provides the most relevant search results.

Directory assistance is self-explanatory. The local Comptroller's office is usually the office that handles Tax Deeds. If they do not, they should be able to point you in the right direction. Make sure you specify Tax Deeds only, not Tax Liens.

By law, the office advertising the Tax Deed sale must do so in the form of a public notice. The most common form of public notice is advertising in a newspaper with at least a minimum circulation.

Some counties are more technologically advanced than others. Most small counties do not list information on a website, do not have a website, or do not frequently update their information. At the very least, they must advertise Tax Deed sales through a public newspaper. Once you contact the Office of the Comptroller, they should be able to inform you which local newspapers they advertise Tax Deed sales in.

If you are unsuccessful with these suggestions please visit www.taxdeedbook.com. This site should provide you will all the information you need.

Tax Deed File

Now that you have located the office where Tax Deed Sales are held, you will need to find the Tax Deed files. These files may be viewed either in paper form where you physically look at all the documents in the file, or electronically online. When you call or go to the Tax Deed office, they will inform you where and how to view these files. These files will have many pages and subgroups.

Each county is different, but for the most part, here is a list of the categories in each file:

DR 513 (sometimes named something else)

Tax Sale Certification

Title Search Report

Payment Requests

Mailing Documents

Other Documents

Some of these categories are self-explanatory. We will need to read each one in detail. Your county may consolidate some of these items and may not call them by the names we are using in the book; however, all the information should be in the file.

The following examples contain black outlines corresponding to the items we explain below. Some personal information is blacked out for privacy reasons.

DR 513

This file is a government form that should give most of the important information such as:

Parcel ID or Alt Key

Tax Certificate Number

Application Date of Tax Deed

Applicant Name and Address

Date of Certificate Sale

Face Amount

Interest Due

Fees

Minimum or Open Bid Amount

```
FORM 513                                          APPLICATION / SALE DATE
(R. 12/00)        TAX COLLECTOR'S CERTIFICATION   1/26/2003
```

This is to certify that the holder listed below of Tax Sale Certificate Number 01-012056.000, Issued MAY 25 2001 and which encumbers the following described property in the County of ORANGE, State of Florida, to-wit: 13-23-30-1250-02030

```
TAX DEED APPLICANT:                       LEGAL DESCRIPTION:
    OVERBROOK INVESTMENT CLUB              CHARLIN PARK THIRD ADDITION 2/30
                                          LOT 203
    FT WALTON BCH FL 32547                OR B&P 4891/0779,ON 02-02-95,INST QC
```

has surrendered same in my office and made written application for tax deed in accordance with Florida Statutes. I Certify that the following tax certificates, interest, ownership and encumbrance report fee, and Tax Collector's fees have been paid. *Rec. 4-1524 +25*

Certificates Owned by Applicant and Filed in Connection With This Application:

CERT. NO.	DATE OF SALE	TAX YEAR	FACE AMOUNT	INTEREST	T.C. FEE	TOTAL
01-012056.000	05/25/01	2000	1,441.90	648.86	.00	2,090.76

Certificates Redeemed by Applicant in Connection With This Tax Deed Application:

CERT. NO.	DATE OF SALE	TAX YEAR	FACE AMOUNT	INTEREST	T.C. FEE	TOTAL
00-011432.000	05/19/00	1999	1,408.17	887.15	6.25	2,301.57
02-012433.000	05/24/02	2001	1,570.84	282.75	6.25	1,859.84
03-013108.000	05/23/03	2002	1,345.20	67.26	6.25	1,418.71

```
1.  Total of all Certificates in Applicant's Possession and Cost
    of the Certificates Redeemed by Applicant or included (County)    7,670.88
2.  Total of Delinquent Taxes Paid by Tax Deed Applicant........         .00
3.  Total of Current Taxes Paid by Tax Deed Applicant.......2,002.   1,246.67
4.  Ownership and Encumbrance Report Fee.....................         115.00
5.  Tax Deed Application Fee.................................          15.00
6.  Total Interest Accrued by Tax Collector per Florida Statutes..
7.  Total (Lines 1 - 6)......................................       9,047.55
8.  Clerk of Court Statutory Fee for Processing Tax Deed:........         .00
9.  Clerk of Court Certified Mail Charge.....................            .00
10. Clerk of Court Advertising Charge.......................            .00
11. Clerk of Court Recording Fee for Certificate of Notice......         .00
12. Sheriff's Fee...........................................            .00
13. Interest Computed by Clerk of Court Per Florida Statutes.....         .00
14. Total (Lines 8 - 13)....................................            .00
15. Statutory (Opening) Bid; Total of Lines 7 and 14........       9,047.55
16. Redemption Fee..........................................           .25
17. Total Amount to Redeem..................................       9,053.80
```

```
*Done this the    9    day of    December        , 20  03

    TAX COLLECTOR OF ORANGE COUNTY

        By    G. Morales
```

*This certification must be surrendered to the Clerk of Court no later than ten days after this date.

EXHIBIT A

First, this document shows us the parcel ID number, 13-23-30-1250-02030. This number is important in locating the property address.

We need this information to research the property, to see if we are interested in bidding.

The next number in line 1 show the amount the lien holder is owed and how many lien certificates they own. In this case, they are owed $7,670.88.

The remaining lines show us other fees associated with the sale of the property. Finally, line 17 gives us a total amount, which is the "minimum bid". This amount is $9,053.80.

Tax Certification Information

This document is a copy or an original document of the <u>Tax Lien</u> sale. It will have the certificate number, date of sale, buyer's name, legal description of the property, and the interest calculations with fees.

DR-509
R. 07/93

TAX SALE CERTIFICATE NO. | 012056.000 |
This Certificate will be void seven years from date of issue.

STATE OF FLORIDA   OFFICE OF TAX COLLECTOR

I,_____ E A R L   K.   W O O D _____, Tax Collector for the County of

_____ ORANGE _____, in the State of Florida, do hereby certify that

I did, at public auction, pursuant to notice given by law as required, on this the____ 25 ____ day of

_____ MAY _____, 2001 ___, issue to
(year)

OVERBROOK INVESTMENT CLUB

a tax sale certificate covering the parcel(s) hereinafter described for the sum of ____ 1,441 ____ DOLLARS and ____ 90 ____ CENTS, said sum being the amount due for taxes, interest, costs and charges of the described parcel(s) for the year ____ 2000 ____, that the above named purchaser of this certificate or assigns will therefore be entitled to apply for a Tax Deed of such parcel(s) in accordance with the law unless the same shall be redeemed within such periods of time as are provided by law, by payment of such amount and interest thereon from the date of this certificate at the rate of eighteen percent per annum, if purchased by the county or eighteen percent per annum (or at such lower rate of interest as may be bid by any purchaser other than the county).

DUPLICATE CERTIFICATE

Said parcel(s) are described as follows:
                                 EXEMPTION MST 332 2719

PARCEL NUMBER	TYPE	VALUE	TAXABLE VALUE	CODE	ACRES
	NOEXM	0			
13-23-30-1250-02030		59,316		UNINCORPORATED	

DESCRIPTION:
CHARLIN PARK THIRD ADDITION 2/30   LOT 203
OR B&P 4891/0779,ON 02-02-95,INST QC

In the County of _____ ORANGE _____, State of Florida.
The interest rate bid at the sale pursuant to Chapter 197, Florida Statutes, was ____ 18.00 ____ percent.
WITNESS my hand at _____ ORLANDO _____, Florida, this ___ day of
_____ JUNE _____, 2001 ___.
(year)

EXHIBIT B-1   Signature: *Earl K. Wood* _____, Tax Collector

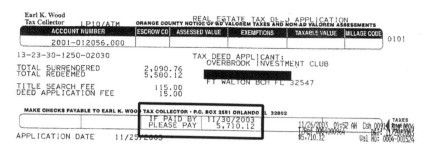

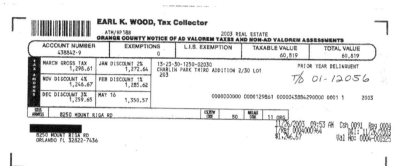

PAY ONLY WITH CASHIERS CHECK, MONEY ORDER, OR CASH

EXHIBIT B-2

Earl K. Wood
Tax Collector   LP10/ATM   ORANGE COUNTY NOTICE OF AD VALOREM TAXES AND NON-AD VALOREM ASSESSMENTS

1999 REAL ESTATE TAX CERTIFICATE

ACCOUNT NUMBER	ESCROW CD	ASSESSED VALUE	EXEMPTIONS	TAXABLE VALUE	MILLAGE CODE	
2000-011432.000	080	57,478	0	57,478	11 U	9901

13-23-30-1250-02030
CHARLIN PARK THIRD ADDITION 2/30
LOT 203
OR B&P 4891/0779,ON 02-02-95,INST QC   ███████ MT RIGA RD
8250   ORLANDO   FL   32822-7436

CERTIFICATE HOLDER:
MARSH GEORGE B OR
MARSH ISABEL J OR GLENN P MARSH

MAKE CHECKS PAYABLE TO EARL K. WOOD TAX COLLECTOR • P.O. BOX 2551 ORLANDO FL 32802

FACE VALUE	INT %	IF PAID BY	11/30/2003			TAXES DUE IF PAID IN
1,408.17	18.00	PLEASE PAY	2,301.57			

TAX DEED APPLIED FOR BY:
OVERBROOK INVESTMENT CLUB

Earl K. Wood
Tax Collector   LP10/ATM   ORANGE COUNTY NOTICE OF AD VALOREM TAXES AND NON-AD VALOREM ASSESSMENTS

2000 REAL ESTATE TAX CERTIFICATE

ACCOUNT NUMBER	ESCROW CD	ASSESSED VALUE	EXEMPTIONS	TAXABLE VALUE	MILLAGE CODE	
2001-012056.000	080	59,316	0	59,316	11 U	0001

13-23-30-1250-02030
CHARLIN PARK THIRD ADDITION 2/30
LOT 203
OR B&P 4891/0779,ON 02-02-95,INST QC   8250 MT RIGA RD
ORLANDO   FL   32822-7436

CERTIFICATE HOLDER:
OVERBROOK INVESTMENT CLUB

MAKE CHECKS PAYABLE TO EARL K. WOOD TAX COLLECTOR • P.O. BOX 2551 ORLANDO FL 32802

FACE VALUE	INT %	IF PAID BY	11/30/2003			TAXES DUE IF PAID IN
1,441.90	18.00	PLEASE PAY	2,090.76			

SURRENDERED BY:
OVERBROOK INVESTMENT CLUB

Earl K. Wood
Tax Collector   LP10/ATM   ORANGE COUNTY NOTICE OF AD VALOREM TAXES AND NON-AD VALOREM ASSESSMENTS

2001 REAL ESTATE TAX CERTIFICATE

ACCOUNT NUMBER	ESCROW CD	ASSESSED VALUE	EXEMPTIONS	TAXABLE VALUE	MILLAGE CODE	
2002-012433.000	080	58,955	0	58,955	11 U	0101

13-23-30-1250-02030
CHARLIN PARK THIRD ADDITION 2/30
LOT 203
OR B&P 4891/0779,ON 02-02-95,INST QC   8250 MT RIGA RD
ORLANDO   FL   32822-7436

CERTIFICATE HOLDER:
MIRZA JAVED

MAKE CHECKS PAYABLE TO EARL K. WOOD TAX COLLECTOR • P.O. BOX 2551 ORLANDO FL 32802

FACE VALUE	INT %	IF PAID BY	11/30/2003			TAXES DUE IF PAID IN
1,570.84	18.00	PLEASE PAY	1,859.84			

TAX DEED APPLIED FOR BY:
OVERBROOK INVESTMENT CLUB

Earl K. Wood
Tax Collector   LP10/ATM   ORANGE COUNTY NOTICE OF AD VALOREM TAXES AND NON-AD VALOREM ASSESSMENTS

2002 REAL ESTATE TAX CERTIFICATE

ACCOUNT NUMBER	ESCROW CD	ASSESSED VALUE	EXEMPTIONS	TAXABLE VALUE	MILLAGE CODE	
2003-013108.000	080	57,387	0	57,387	11 U	0201

13-23-30-1250-02030
CHARLIN PARK THIRD ADDITION 2/30
LOT 203
OR B&P 4891/0779,ON 02-02-95,INST QC   8250 MOUNT RIGA RD
ORLANDO   FL   32822-7436

CERTIFICATE HOLDER:
WHEELER JANIS HILLMAN

MAKE CHECKS PAYABLE TO EARL K. WOOD TAX COLLECTOR • P.O. BOX 2551 ORLANDO FL 32802

FACE VALUE	INT %	IF PAID BY	11/30/2003			TAXES DUE IF PAID IN
1,345.20	8.00	PLEASE PAY	1,418.71			

TAX DEED APPLIED FOR BY:
OVERBROOK INVESTMENT CLUB

EXHIBIT B-3

NOTICE TO ⌒ COLLECTOR OF APPLICATION ⌒OR TAX DEED

DR-512
R. 05/88

TO: Tax Collector of _____ *Orange* _____ County:

In accordance with the Florida Statutes, I, ███████████████████, holder of the following tax sale certificate hereby surrender same to the Tax Collector and make tax deed application thereon:

CERT. NO.	DATE	LEGAL DESCRIPTION
01 - 12056	5-25-01	13-23- 30-1250- 02030
		Charlin Park Third Add
		Lot 203

I agree to pay all delinquent taxes, redeem all outstanding tax certificates not in my possession, pay any omitted taxes, and pay current taxes, if due, covering the land, and pay any interest earned (a) on tax certificates not in my possession, (b) on omitted taxes or (c) on delinquent taxes. I also agree to pay all tax collector's fees, ownership and encumbrance report costs, clerk of the court costs, charges and fees and sheriff's costs, if applicable. Attached is the above-mentioned tax sale certificate on which this application is based and all other certificates of the same legal description which are in my possession.

████████████████████   _11- 20 - 03_
Applicant's Signature   Date

EXHIBIT B-4

We are not as interested in these documents. They show the company or individual that purchased the Tax Lien, the date it was acquired, and the interest rate it is accruing.

The final document shows the owner of the certificate applying for the Tax Deed to force the sale of the property because real estate taxes have not been paid by the property owner. This was signed on 11/20/03.

Title Search Report

Some Counties execute a title search for each property that is to be auctioned. The title search provides the County with information about additional liens (such as mortgages) and other money owed.

Once the liens have been identified, the County can send out notices to the lien holders (individuals or companies) informing them of the proposed Tax Deed auction. This is very important, because it is the duty of the County to give reasonable notice to anyone who has interest in the property. Notice is also given in the local news publication.

The County does this because if interested parties do not receive proper notice, they have time after the sale to dispute the sale, which can potentially null and void the sale. If this were to happen, the bidder's money would be refunded, and the property would be re-auctioned after the dispute was resolved. The mere fact that the County performs this title search is of great benefit to you. It provides you with valuable information regarding the property you are interested in, plus it saves you money. Other methods of purchasing properties from government type auctions do not offer any type of title search. Foreclosures are a good example of this. If you purchase any type of real estate without performing a title search, you are at risk of making a very expensive mistake. Running title searches for each auction property of interest can be expensive, so here you can see one of the benefits from purchasing properties at a Tax Deed auction.

Example

A property is scheduled for auction at a Tax Deed sale. ABC Mortgage Company holds the original mortgage on the property. If ABC Mortgage Company doesn't receive notice of the auction, they may be able to dispute the sale, making it null and void. The county would then have to re-list the property and go through the process again.

The reason the County gives notice of the sale to any individual or company who holds an interest in the property is so that they have the opportunity to pay off the back due tax amount prior to the auction date, thereby stopping the sale.

FIDELITY TITLE & GUARANTY CO.

ESTABLISHED 1883

A wholly owned subsidiary of First American Title Insurance Company

TITLE INFORMATION COMPILED FOR EARL K. WOOD
TAX COLLECTOR, ORANGE COUNTY, FLORIDA
RELATIVE TO TAX DEED SALES

Tax Sale Certificate No.   01-012056.000

Fidelity Title File No.   03.00851Q/390295

Legal Description:

Lot 203, CHARLIN PARK, THIRD ADDITION, according to the plat thereof as recorded in Plat Book 2, Page 30, Public Records of Orange County, Florida.

Title Vested In:

▮▮▮▮ by virtue of that certain Quit Claim Deed filed May 12, 1995 in Official Records Book 4891, Page 779, Public Records of Orange County, Florida.

Encumbrances:

1. Mortgage executed by ▮▮▮▮▮▮▮▮▮▮ in favor of First Union National Bank of Florida dated May 31, 1996 and filed June 25, 1996 in Official Records Book 5078, Page 4557, in the original amount of $50,000.00, Public Records of Orange County, Florida.

Other Information:

NONE

Lien and Judgment Search (includes Federal) made on:

▮▮▮▮▮

THIS TITLE SEARCH REPORT EXCLUDES ALL MATTERS RELATIVE TO ALL TAX CERTIFICATES OR TAXES.

THIS INFORMATION COMPILED AS OF: November 25, 2003 at 4:00 p.m.

No easements, conditions, restrictions, reservations, or limitations on use of any kind, have been included herein, as directed. This Title Search Report ("Report") is a search limited to the Official Records Books as defined in Sections 28.0001(1) and 28.222, Florida Statutes. The foregoing Report accurately reflects matters recorded and indexed in the Official Records Books of Orange County, Florida, affecting title to the property described therein. Liability for any incorrect information contained in this Report is limited (1) to the person or entity to whom the Report is directed, and (2) to a maximum of $1,000.00 pursuant to Section 627.7843(3), Florida Statutes. This Report is not an opinion of title, title insurance policy, warranty of title, or any other assurance as to the status of title. This Report is limited to applicable: Mortgages, liens, and claims of liens, judgments, federal tax liens, bankruptcy matters, death certificates, options, contracts of any kind, court orders and decrees, divorce matters, tax warrants, incompetency and probate matters which may affect title to the property described, herein.

FIDELITY TITLE AND GUARANTY COMPANY

BY: ▮▮▮▮▮▮▮▮▮▮

EXHIBIT C-1

QUITCLAIM DEED

Orange Co FL ██████
06/18/96 02:51:00pm
OR Bk 4891 Pg 779
Rec 6.00 DOC 38.90

Record Verified - Martha O. Haynie

THIS QUITCLAIM DEED, Executed this 2 day of FEB. , 1995 first party,

to: ██

Whose post office address is █████ Orlando, Florida 32807 to second party:

███████████ whose post office address is 8250 Mt. Riga Rd., Orlando, Florida.

32822.

WITNESSETH, That the said first party, for good consideration and for the sum
of TEN DOLLARS ($10.00) paid by the second party, the receipt whereof is hereby
acknowledged, does hereby remise, release and quitclaim unto the said second party
forever, all the right, title, interest and claim which the said first party has in and to the
following described parcel of land, and improvements and appurtenances thereto in the
County of Orange, State of Florida to wit:

LOT 203, CHARLIN PARK, THIRD ADDITION,

ACCORDING TO THE PLAT THEREOF, AS RECORDED IN PLAT

BOOK 2, PAGE 30, PUBLIC RECORDS OF ORANGE COUNTY, FLORIDA.

IN WITNESS WHEREOF, The said first party has signed and sealed these
presents the day and year first above written. Signed, sealed and delivered in presence of:

█████████████████ residing at ORLANDO, FLORIDA

█████████████████████ residing at ORLANDO, FLORIDA

STATE OF FLORIDA

COUNTY OF ORANGE

On FEBRUARY 2, 1995, before me, the undersigned Notary Public in and for said
State, personally appeared ████████████ who has produced S520-168-58-219
identification and proved to be the person who executed the within Quitclaim Deed.

Notary Public-State of Florida
My Commission Expires:

EXHIBIT C-2

MORTGAGE

THIS MORTGAGE, is made this 31st day of May 1996 , between the Mortgagor,

(herein "Borrower") and the Mortgagee, FIRST UNION NATIONAL BANK OF FLORIDA, a national banking association organized and existing under the laws of the United States of America, whose address is 214 N. Hogan Street, 8th Floor, Jacksonville, Fl 32202-4240 (herein "Lender").

$ 50,000.00 Lender has agreed to extend credit to borrower, from time to time, in a total principal amount not to exceed pursuant to the terms of that certain Prime Equity Line Application and Prime Equity Line Agreement and (herein "Agreement"), of even date herewith, executed and delivered by Borrower to Lender, which terms and conditions are incorporated into this mortgage, which Agreement provides for repayment of such advances in monthly installments, together with interest as provided therein. The total of advances may increase and decrease from time to time but shall never exceed the face amount of this Mortgage, as aforesaid, and shall be paid in full on or before a date which is twenty (20) years from the date of this Mortgage.

TO SECURE to Lender (a) the repayment of the indebtedness evidenced by the Agreement, with interest thereon, the payment of all other sums, with interest thereon, advanced in accordance herewith to protect the security of this Mortgage and the performance of the covenants and agreements of Borrower herein contained, and (b) the repayment of any future advance, with interest thereon, made to Borrower by Lender (herein "Future Advances"), Borrower does hereby mortgage, grant and convey to Lender the following described property located in the County of ORANGE , State of Florida.

LOT 203, CHARLIN PARK, THIRD ADDITION, ACCORDING TO THE PLAT THEREOF AS RECORDED IN PLAT BOOK 2, PAGE 30, PUBLIC RECORDS OF ORANGE COUNTY, FLORIDA.

which has the address of 8250 MOUNT RIGA RD, ORLANDO, FL 32822 , (herein "Property Address");
(Property Address)

TOGETHER with all the improvements now or hereafter erected on the property, and all easements, rights, appurtenances, rents, royalties, mineral, oil and gas rights and profits, water, water rights, and water stock, and all fixtures now or hereafter attached to the property, all of which, including replacements and additions thereto, shall be deemed to be and remain a part of the property covered by this Mortgage; and all of the foregoing, together with said property (or the leasehold estate if this Mortgage is on a leasehold) are herein referred to as the mortgaged property.

TO HAVE AND TO HOLD the said mortgaged property unto the Lender, in fee simple.

AND BORROWER does hereby fully warrant the title to the said mortgaged property and will defend the same against lawful claims of all persons whomsoever.

AND BORROWER warrants and represents to Lender as follows:

A. The title to said property is held as indicated hereinabove.

B. That the aforesaid property is in the exclusive possession of Borrower(s).

Page 1 of 4

EXHIBIT C-3

B. That the aforesaid property is in the exclusive possession of Borrower(s).

C. That no labor has been performed or materials furnished within three (3) months last past in connection with any repairs, alterations or work done upon said premises and that there are no unpaid bills or indebtedness or any labor done or materials furnished at any time upon or in connection with said premises which could be or out of which could arise any materialmen's or merchanic's liens against said premises or any part thereof, and that no notice of commencement of any improvements upon said property has been given, posted or recorded.

D. That Borrower(s) have not executed and do not know of any instrument affecting the title to the said premises, including judgments against the Borrower(s) or their predecessors in title to said premises, whether or not recorded, except as follows:

_____N/A_____

OR BK 5078 Pg 4558
Orange Co FL 5663915

AND BORROWER further covenants with Lender as follows:

1. To pay when due all sums provided in said agreement and any renewal, extension or modification thereof, and is this mortgage.

2. To pay when due, and without requiring any notice from Lender, all taxes, assessments of any type or nature, and other charges levied or assessed against the mortgaged property hereby encumbered, or any interest of Lender therein, and produce receipts therefore upon demand. To immediately pay and discharge any claim, lien or encumbrance against the mortgaged property which may be or become superior to this mortgage (unless herein above specifically excepted) and to permit no default or delinquency on any other lien, encumbrance or charge against the mortgaged property.

3. To keep the mortgaged property insured against loss or damage by fire, and such other hazards in form and amounts and for such periods, as may be required by the lender, and to pay promptly when due all premiums of such insurance. The policies and renewals of said insurance shall be held by the Lender, and shall have attached thereto loss payable clauses in favor of, and in a form acceptable to the Lender.

4. To maintain the mortgaged property in good condition, and repair, including but not limited to the making of such repairs as Lender may from time to time determine to be necessary, for the preservation of the same; to commit, suffer or permit no waste of said property or the improvements thereon.

5. To comply with all laws, ordinances, regulations, covenants, conditions and restrictions affecting the mortgaged property and not to suffer or permit any violation thereof.

6. If the borrower fails to pay any claim, lien or encumbrance which is superior to, in parity with or subordinate to this mortgage, or to pay when due any tax or assessment or insurance premium, or to keep the premises in repair, or shall commit, suffer or permit waste, or if there be commenced any action at law or equity or any proceeding affecting the mortgaged property or the title thereto, the Lender, at its option, may pay said claim, lien, encumbrance, tax, assessment or premium, may make such repairs and counsel therein, and take such action as the Lender deems advisable, and for any of said purposes, the Lender may advance such sums of money, including all costs, reasonable attorneys fees and other items of expense as it deems necessary: Nothing herein contained shall be construed as requiring the Lender to advance monies for any of the purposes aforesaid, and the advance of such monies for such purposes shall in no way waive or affect the Lender's right of foreclosure or any other right or remedy hereunder.

7. Borrower will pay to Lender, immediately and without demand, all sums of money advanced by Lender pursuant to this mortgage, including all costs, reasonable attorneys fees, whether or not legal action has actually been filed, and other items of expense, together with interest on each such advancement at the rate provided in the Agreement, and all such sums and interest thereon shall be secured hereby.

8. If default is made in performance of any of Borrower's obligations, covenants or agreements hereunder or as stated in the Agreement, all of the indebtedness secured hereby shall become and be immediately due and payable at the option of the Lender. Lender may avail itself of all rights and remedies at law or in equity, and this mortgage may be foreclosed, and borrower shall pay all costs and expenses thereof, including the cost of securing abstracts or other evidence of the status of title to mortgaged property, and reasonable attorneys fees.

In addition to the remedies provided for breach of certain conditions of the Mortgage, Lender may declare Borrower in default under this Mortgage if any of the following events occur: (1) if Borrower fails to make the payment within 10 days of the due date; (2) if Borrower writes Prime Equity Line Checks in excess of the available credit limit or the maximum credit limit; (3) if a petition is filed or other proceedings started under the federal Bankruptcy code or any state insolvency status or if a receiver is appointed or writ or order of attachment, Levy or judgement is issued against Borrower or the Property meets or income that affects Borrower's ability to repay the Agreement in accordance with the term of the agreement or that adversely affects Lender's security rights in the Property; (4) if Borrower permits any other lienholder to gain or appear to gain priority over Lender except whatever first mortgage deed of trust or deed to secure debt is outstanding on the Property at the time of recording of Lender's mortgage to secure the Agreement; (5) if the Property is condemned or is totally or partially destroyed by fire or other hazards or any proceeding is commenced which materially affects Lenders Interest in the Property; (6) if the secured note for any prior mortgage deed of trust or deed to secure debt or lien on the real Property is in default by failure of Borrower to pay principal, interest, charges, fees, escrow items, or the commencement of a foreclosure proceeding or collection action that adversely affects Lender's interest in the Property; (7) if Lender believes in good faith that Borrower has allowed the Property to deteriorate, committed waste, or destructively used or failed to maintain the Property; (8) if Borrower commits fraud or misrepresents any information in the loan application, the agreement or the mortgage at any time; (9) if Borrower fails to disclose any known environmental condition or hazard which adversely affects Lenders security interest in the Property; (10) if Borrower fails to maintain adequate insurance coverage on the Property naming mortgagees as insured; (11) if Borrower fails to pay taxes and assessments on the Property that results in a filing of a lien senior to Lender's lien that impairs Lender's security interest in the Property; or (12) if Borrower transfers title to Property without Lender's consent as set forth in the terms of this Mortgage or transfer of title occurs due to any death or by governmental action, however, Borrower understands Lender will not terminate the Agreement and accelerate payment if such action is prohibited by federal law as of the date of the Agreement.

EXHIBIT C-4

9. No delay by Lender in exercising any right or remedy hereunder or otherwise afforded by law shall operate as waiver thereof or preclude the exercise during the continuance of any default hereunder. No waiver by Lender of any default shall constitute a waiver of or consent to subsequent defaults.

10. Without affecting the liability of any person (other than any person released pursuant to the provisions of this paragraph) for payment of any indebtedness secured hereby and without affecting the priority or extent of the lien hereof upon any property not specifically released pursuant hereto, Lender may at any time and from time to time without notice and without limitation as to any legal right or privilege of Lender: (a) release any person liable for payment of any indebtedness secured hereby (b) extend the time or agree to alter the terms of payment of any of the indebtedness (c) accept additional security of any kind (d) release any property securing the indebtedness or (e) consent to the creation of any easement on or over the mortgaged property or any covenants restricting use or occupancy thereof.

11. Any agreement hereafter made by Borrower and Lender pursuant to this Mortgage shall be superior to the rights of the holder of any intervening lien or encumbrance.

OR Bk 5078 Pg 4559
Orange Co FL 5643915

12. Borrower hereby waives all right of homestead or other exemption in the property subject to this Mortgage, not including Homestead Tax Exemption.

13. The mailing of written notice or demand addressed to the Borrower at the last address actually furnished to the Lender or at such mortgaged property and mailed postage prepaid, by United States mail, shall be sufficient notice or demand in any case arising under this instrument and required by the provisions or by law.

14. The covenants and agreements herein contained shall bind and the benefits and advantages shall inure to the respective heirs, executors, administrators, successors, and assigns of the parties hereto. All covenants, agreements and undertakings shall be joint and several.

15. This Mortgage is granted to secure future advances from the Lender to the Borrower made, at the option of the lender, within twenty (20) years of the date hereof. The unpaid principal balance of the indebtedness hereby secured, exclusive of disbursements made by the Lender for taxes, levies, assessments and insurance and exclusive of accrued interest, shall never at one time exceed the principal amount of the Agreement, as shown on the face hereof.

16. Pursuant to Section 697.04(1)(b), Florida Statutes, Mortgagor hereby gives notice that the maximum principal amount secured by any Mortgage senior to this Mortgage shall hereafter be limited to the principal balance hereof outstanding as of the date of this notice, which Mortgagor certifies to be in an amount not greater than N/A

_____ ($_____).

17. If any mortgage senior to this Mortgage secures revolving or open end credit, mortgagor hereby certifies that all credit cards, checks and other devices used to obtain future advances under said Mortgage have this date been surrendered to the Senior Mortgagee.

18. Mortgagor further certifies that a copy of this notice has been furnished to any Senior Mortgagee this date by certified mail as required in the above referenced statute and by any other form of notice as may be required under the provisions of any senior mortgage.

19. Transfer of the Property or a beneficial Interest in Borrower. Assumption. If all or any part of the property or any interest in it is sold or transferred (or if a beneficial interest in Borrower is sold or transferred and Borrower is not a natural person) without Lender's prior written consent, Lender may, at Lender's option, declare all the sums secured by this Mortgage to be immediately due and payable. However, this option shall not be exercised by Lender if exercise is prohibited by Federal law as of the date of this Mortgage.

If Lender exercises this option, Lender shall give Borrower notice of acceleration. The notice shall provide a period of not less than 30 days from the date the notice is delivered or mailed within which Borrower must pay all sums secured by the Security instrument. If Borrower fails to pay these sums prior to the expiration of this period, Lender may invoke any remedies permitted by this Mortgage without further notice or demand on Borrower.

This Mortgage may not be assumed by a purchaser without the Lender's consent. If an assumption is allowed, the Lender may charge an assumption fee and require the person(s) assuming the loan to pay additional charges as authorized by law.

20. In case of a conflict between the terms of the Agreement and this Mortgage governing remedies on default or termination of advances, the priority of controlling terms shall be the Agreement and then this Mortgage.

21. Additional terms and conditions: Exhibit 1, Condominium Rider; Exhibit 2, Planned Unit Development Rider (if attached hereto are made a part hereof).

Page 3 of 4

(6043) FL Mortgage

EXHIBIT C-5

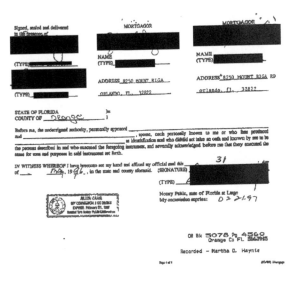

EXHIBIT C-6

EXHIBIT C-7

This document shows us the legal description of the property to be auctioned. Remember that most county documents will not give you a mailing address like you and I are used to. They use legal descriptions and parcel IDs.

This document shows us encumbrances, or liens, on the property. In this case there is a mortgage in the amount of $50,000.

The following documents will usually be a trail of ownership and mortgages or liens.

The important items to search for are going to be government liens that may be difficult to remove from the property, such as IRS liens.

We see in this file they have included a copy of the plat map. We can use the legal description to locate the property. Not all title reports will have copies of the plat maps.

Payment Requests

This section deals with the actual notices and letters that are sent out to the owners on record as of the filing date. The Comptroller's Office tries to locate the owner and serve them with a notice of sale. Generally, the owner of record is served with official papers by the local sheriff. This is the "checks and balances" part of the property file that contains evidence that the government attempted to provide the owner with adequate notice of sale.

There are many times when the owner does not get served. Here are some of those reasons:

The owner is deceased

The owner has moved

The owner has sold the property and the deed was not recorded

The owner's address on file with the county is incorrect

The owner was involved in a divorce and the ex-spouse is not forwarding mail

The owner is incarcerated

The owner no longer lives in the United States and is unreachable

The owner did not leave an address on file with the county

The property is vacant land, and the county does not have a residential address for the owner

There are many other reasons, but in our experience, those are the most common.

3713

WARNING

There are unpaid taxes on the property which you own or in which you have a legal interest. The property will be sold at public auction on Jul-06-2004 unless the back taxes are paid. To make arrangements for payment, or to receive further information, contact the Orange County Comptroller's Tax Deed Office at 401 South Rosalind Avenue, Orlando, FL 32801 or by telephone at (407) 836-5116.

Note: This covers taxes for the following years: 2003, 2002, 2001, 2000, and 1999

NOTICE OF APPLICATION FOR TAX DEED

NOTICE IS HEREBY GIVEN that OVERBROOK INVESTMENT CLUB, the holder of the following certificates has filed said certificates for a TAX DEED to be issued thereon. The Certificate numbers and years of issuance, the description of the property, and the names in which it was assessed are as follows:

CERTIFICATE NUMBER: 12056   **YEAR OF ISSUANCE: 2001**

DESCRIPTION OF PROPERTY:
CHARLIN PARK THIRD ADDITION 2/30 LOT 203 OR B&P 4891/0779 ON 02-02-95 INST QC
PARCEL ID # 13-23-30-1250-02030

Name in which assessed: █████████

ALL of said property being in the County of Orange, State of Florida. Unless such certificate or certificates shall be redeemed according to law the property described in such certificate or certificates will be sold to the highest bidder at **401 South Rosalind Avenue, Orlando, Florida 32801**, on the 06th day of July, 2004 at **10:00 a.m.**

Dated: April 29, 2004

MARTHA O. HAYNIE, County Comptroller,
Orange County, Florida

By: C Willis
Deputy Comptroller

AMOUNT NECESSARY TO REDEEM:
$ 10,492.71 **This amount is subject to change**
(CASH, CASHIERS CHECK or MONEY ORDER made payable to ORANGE COUNTY TAX COLLECTOR)

Send payment to:
    Orange County Tax Collector
    200 South Orange Ave.
    16th Floor
    Orlando, Florida 32801

Revised: 03/14/2003

EXHIBIT D-1

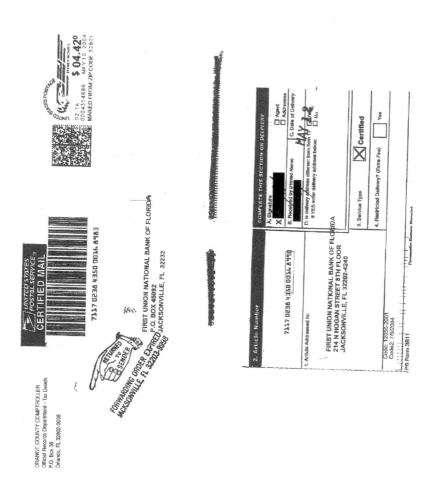

EXHIBIT D-2

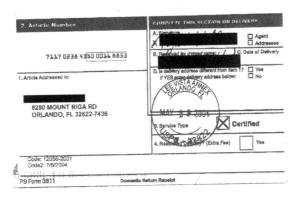

EXHIBIT D-3

PERSONS TO NOTIFY OF PENDING TAX DEED APPLICATION TAKEN /NO
FROM FIDELITY TAX SEARCH 30 4

CERTIFICATE: 12056.000   HOMESTEAD PROPERTY:
YEAR: 2001   NOT HOMESTEAD PROPERTY: X
                                             VALUE: 60,819

LAST ASSESSED PARTY ON TAX ROLL: — WARRANTY DEED: Quit Claim Deed
                    ✓/INO   4891/779
8250 MOUNT RIGA RD
ORLANDO   FL 32822-7436
                                        808 Pablo Ln.
                                        Orlando, FL. 32807
MORTGAGES: 5878/4557   Also:
  10 ✓First Union National Bank of Florida   10 P.O. Box 45092 •
     214 N. Hogan Street 8th floor   Jacksonville, FL 32232
     Jacksonville, FL. 32202-4240

OTHER LIEN HOLDERS OF RECORD:

5078/4557

8250 Mount Riga Rd.
Orlando FL 32822

THIS IS AN ATTACHMENT TO THE TAX COLLECTOR'S CERTIFICATION

EXHIBIT D-4

TAX DEED SALE FOR JULY 6, 2004

71170238435000168853 12056-2001
8250 MOUNT RIGA RD
ORLANDO FL 32822-7436

71170238435000168983 12056-1998
FIRST UNION NATIONAL
BANK OF FLORIDA
P.O. BOX 45092
JACKSONVILLE FL 32232

71170238435000169041 12056-2001
8250 MOUNT RIGA RD
ORLANDO FL 32822

71170238435000168990 12056-2001
FIRST UNION NATIONAL
BANK OF FLORIDA
214 N HOGAN STREET 8TH FLOOR
JACKSONVILLE FL 32202-4240

EXHIBIT D-5

These documents are the final documents sent out to the owner(s) of record and lien holders of the property before going to the auction. Anyone who showed up in the title report that may have an interest in the property must be given notice of the sale.

The County keeps track of these documents in case a person or company tries to dispute the sale. The County can prove they made every attempt to contact the owner and lien holders.

Mailing Documents/Public Notice

This section usually contains the proof that documents were mailed or delivered by the sheriff. Copies of payments or checks are usually posted here.

The amount of paperwork here is usually excessive, and we did not see a reason to include it in the book. Instead, we are showing you another important form, which is the actual 'notice of sale' ad placed in the local newspaper.

EXHIBIT E

Other Documents

Any other documents that are relevant to the property or its owners are posted here. You may find nothing, or you may find hundreds of pages. This section is important because it can provide you with situational information regarding the property and the owners. Carefully look through this section for bankruptcy information. Bankruptcies can complicate Tax Deed sales. Generally, we stay away from Tax Deeds that have pending bankruptcies. There are many laws that protect an owner's home when they file for bankruptcy, which may result in complications in the future.

Now that you have some idea of what you will find in the Tax Deed files, through research, we can apply this information to help us to locate real estate deals.

Recorded in Orange County Florida 07/06/2004 11:54:07 AM Martha O. Haynie
O.R. BK/PG 07513/0977 20040426392 AMT .00 Doc Stamp .00

CLERK'S CERTIFICATE

STATE OF FLORIDA
COUNTY OF ORANGE

I, MARTHA O. HAYNIE, County Comptroller, in and for Orange County, Florida, DO HEREBY CERTIFY that:

1. The Proof of Publication of Notice of Tax Deed Sale of Certificate Number 12056-2001 is attached hereto and made part hereof as Exhibit "A".

2. The Notice of Tax Deed Sale of Certificate Number 12056-2001 a copy of which is attached hereto and made a part hereof as Exhibit "B", was mailed on May 10, 2004 to the names and addresses as shown in Exhibit "C" of this particular sale.

3. The Certified Mail Number under which each Notice was mailed is shown by each name and address.

4. No certified notices were sent to those parties shown on the Tax Collector's Certificate which did not have an address and on which an address was not available upon search.

5. The Tax Collector's Certification is attached as Exhibit "D".

Dated at Orlando, Orange County, Florida, on Jul-06-2004.

By: _____
Deputy Comptroller   SEAL

EXHIBIT F

This shows that the Clerk has followed all the procedures to begin the auction.

Recorded in Orange County Florida 07/06/2004 11:54:07 AM Martha O. Haynie
O.R. BK/PG 07613/0982 20040426393 AMT 33,150.00 Doc Stamp 232.40

TAX DEED

STATE OF FLORIDA
COUNTY OF ORANGE

The following Tax Sale Certificate Numbered 12056 issued on **May 25, 2001** in the office of the Tax Collector of this County and application made for the issuance of a tax deed, the applicant having paid or redeemed all other taxes or tax sale certificates on the land described as required by law to be paid or redeemed, and the costs and expenses of this sale, and due notice of sale having been published as required by law, and no person entitled to do so having appeared to redeem said land; such land was on the **06th day of July, 2004**, offered for sale as required by law for cash to the highest bidder and was sold to:

LONDON MERIDIAN INC

ORLANDO, FL 32807
being the highest bidder and having paid the sum of his bid as required by the Laws of Florida.

NOW, this **06th day of July, 2004**, the County of Orange, State of Florida in consideration of the sum of THIRTY THREE THOUSAND ONE HUNDRED FIFTY AND 00 / 100 Dollars **($ 33,150.00)**, being the amount paid pursuant to the Laws of Florida does hereby sell the following lands situated in the County and State and described as follows:

CHARLIN PARK THIRD ADDITION 2/30 LOT 203 OR B&P 4891/0779 ON 02-02-95 INST QC
Parcel ID# 13-23-30-1250-02030

MARTHA O. HAYNIE, COUNTY COMPTROLLER
ORANGE COUNTY, FLORIDA

BY: _____
Deputy County Comptroller
Orange County, Florida

SEAL

WITNESS:

STATE OF FLORIDA
COUNTY OF ORANGE

On this **06th day of July, 2004**, before me, personally appeared **C Willis**, Deputy County Comptroller in and for the State and County aforesaid, who executed the foregoing instrument, and acknowledged the execution of this instrument to be her own free act and deed for the use and purposes therein mentioned, who is personally known to me and who did not take an oath.

Witness my hand and official seal on the date aforesaid.

_____
Notary Public

Tax Deed File Number # 12056-2001

Miroslava Suarez
Commission #DD289699
Expires: Feb 10, 2008
Bonded Thru
Atlantic Bonding Co., Inc.

EXHIBIT G

This is a copy of the Tax Deed showing our company purchased this property for $33,150.00 on 07/06/2004. We sold this property on 03/04/2005 for $60,000.00.

CHAPTER 2

In this chapter, you will learn:

- How to pursue owners pre-auction
- Techniques for finding information
- Understanding GIS Maps
- Researching Tax Deed properties using public records

Pursuing Owners

Congratulations on becoming educated in locating Tax Deeds in your local area! You must now make an important decision. Should I wait for the property to go to auction or should I directly approach the owner before the sale? We prefer waiting for a property to go to sale at auction. Other Tax Deed investors we know prefer the pre-sale approach. That is something you can decide for yourself. If you are comfortable with contacting the owner prior to the sale, this could prove to be highly profitable, as many people do not favor this approach because of the effort involved. In this section, we will cover locating the owner and contacting them, their neighbors, or family.

This presale technique of contacting the owner is very sensitive. Sometimes these owners are in troublesome financial situations and may be embarrassed to discuss this with a stranger. We encourage you to keep an open mind and be respectful of the owner. Try to put yourself in their shoes and imagine the way in which you would want to be approached if you were in the same situation. In approaching the owner, you will need to provide a win-win situation without being threatening, over-promising, or unethical.

Whether your approach is face to face, by phone, certified letter, or through their neighbors, we urge you to exercise the golden rule:

<u>Treat them as you would want to be treated!</u>

We assure you that your results will be more fruitful if you use this approach. Most of the owners you will be dealing with will be facing financial difficulties caused by any number of things. Circumstances such as divorce, bankruptcy, unemployment, or family death may have forced individuals to become past due on their taxes.

Some properties are inherited by family members due to the death of a relative. At times, this inheritance can be unwanted because of the extra expenses involved in owning a second property. These inheritors cannot afford the taxes, and therefore find themselves in awkward situations. Sometimes, the inheritor can afford the property, but burdens with maintenance, upkeep, security, and location can be off-putting. Be sensitive to these circumstances, and you will find the owners really do appreciate your help and understanding.

One of the disadvantages to the presale approach is that you may be looked upon as someone who is trying to take their house from them. We know this is not the case, but the property owners do not. In some cases, property owners do not realize that the County is selling the house for unpaid taxes. However, using logic to reason with someone who is faced with losing their home will not always receive the most welcome responses.

If you are able to turn an owner's unfortunate circumstance into a mutually beneficial situation, you may be looked upon as saint. Don't laugh. It happened to us! (We will explain this later in the book!)

Neighbors

This is one of the most under-used sources of information. It's amazing what the neighbors will tell you, as they like to talk and appear knowledgeable. Let them talk! When they talk, <u>act very interested</u>. Don't interrupt. Talking is one of the most infectious pastimes for some people. The more you let them talk, the more you will discover.

Case Study

In June 2004, we were looking at a property in Kissimmee, FL which was scheduled for tax auction in July 2004. We decided to approach the owners prior to the sale to see if we could help them out of their predicament by purchasing their home from them. As we were parking outside the property to evaluate its condition, the next-door neighbor approached us. Apparently, they had seen several people driving up and down the quiet street, and they wanted to know what was going on. After 30 minutes, the neighbor told us not only the owner's phone number, but also what time they came home from work, their children's names and ages, their place of employment, what kind of car they drove, and the most important piece of information, that they were in big trouble financially! We didn't really ask for this information, we simply let them talk, and talk, and talk! The neighbor also explained that the owners were personal friends of theirs and that they were very ashamed of their financial problems and too embarrassed to ask for help! Amazing! The information the neighbor gave us was very helpful in contacting the owner. This was much more information than we could have gotten out of the owners themselves!

Talking to the neighbors is a delicate skill. Some can be suspicious, protective, uncooperative, or maybe even hostile. We always let the neighbors know our plans of helping the neighborhood by raising the values of the local properties. If we can raise the value of the property across the street, it is a good possibility that the neighbor's property will rise in value as well. We also explain to the neighbors that if the house goes to auction, the property owner can be left homeless, with no financial compensation. If the owner is able to sell the property prior to the auction sale, they can be financially compensated and free of any real estate tax obligations. This gives the owner a chance for a fresh beginning. A neighbor's responsiveness will be a direct reflection of your approach, their mood, your attitude, and your ability to communicate in terms they understand and ask questions they feel comfortable answering.

Older neighbors generally pay attention to what is going on in their neighborhood. Why is this important? They are full of information about who is selling, for how much, why they are selling, etc. Of course, not everyone pays attention to their community, but someone who has been living there for many years is more likely to be observant.

The 'gift of gab' is certainly helpful in extracting information about the neighborhood, the neighbors themselves, and the home values in that specific community.

Telephone

Before you pick up the phone to call a property owner, you have to know how to locate that person's phone number. Most of the time, the owner's phone number is not part of the file you will be viewing in your Comptroller's office or on the internet.

Most property owners can be located in the local phone book or local directory. If you are having a problem locating a person's number, there are multiple online services available. You can try different search engines, such as Google or Yahoo. Over the course of time, you will find these websites offer a plethora of information for tracking down owners or their family members. If you aren't locating the person while searching online, widen your search by using less information.

Try this example

Go to www.google.com and look for a random name in the city you live in or a nearby city. For instance, try Jonathan Williams in Miami, Florida as an example: type "Jonathan Williams Miami FL" into Google's search box. Be sure to include the state abbreviation. After you check out these listings, you may have too many results, or not enough results. You can increase or decrease the amount of information you provide the website. Try "J Williams Miami FL" for more results or "Jon (John) Williams Miami FL" for fewer results. Play around with different spellings, or try just a letter for the first name. Sometimes people use a first and middle initial with the last name.

There are sites and companies that specialize in locating people, phone numbers, addresses, etc. Some work on a pay per name basis, while others are based on monthly fees.

Cold-calling the owner can be very impersonal, and many people become defensive, angry, or suspicious when random people phone. Therefore, be prepared for your calls to go unanswered; and most of all, if your call is answered, be prepared for rejection. We suggest that you practice role-playing with a friend, spouse, or business partner to prepare for any rebuttals or potential conflict.

If you are lucky enough to have the property owner answer the phone, you must be 100% prepared. An owner who hears hesitation in your voice may think you are trying to take advantage of them, resulting in the conversation ending there and then. Remember not to just be 'logical' about the transaction, but truly try to feel for the owner's situation and look for a solution that would benefit you both. Explain to the owner that you are in the real estate business, but you want to make sure he does not lose his home. Some of the things a property owner may say include:

Who is this again?
How did you get my number?
Why are you calling me?
I told you not to call me!
Stop bothering me!

I don't deal with that; you'll have to talk to my husband (or wife)!
What do you mean someone is going to take my home!?
I pay my mortgage on time!
You don't know what you're talking about!

We have heard every excuse under the sun—some real, and some ridiculous. We simply want you to be aware that the investment real estate business is a numbers game. A small percentage of owners will be willing to work out a deal with you prior to the sale, but most will not. Most property owners do not want to speak with investors because of a lack of understanding regarding their situation, or simply because they are ashamed. Also remember if the owner is willing to work with you, then they are also willing to work out a deal with your competitors, so some negotiation will be involved.

Mail

Sending mail to an owner is very easy, unless the owner has moved and is unreachable. Even then, there are forwarding services and tracking services you can use to locate the owners.

Mailing a letter is very simple and straightforward for you; but, unfortunately, a letter is also easy for the recipient to throw away. Since most of the owners are in financial distress, they may be ignoring the mail, especially bills, or anything that appears official. Most property owners who owe money avoid mail like the plague. If you are going to put time and effort into mailing out letters, we highly recommend you find a system, and create a letter that will stand out from the rest. Some people resort to gimmicks when sending letters. We have never used these gimmicks personally, so we cannot comment on whether or not they work. We do know, however, that the many letters we have received from people trying to buy our rental properties tend to go in the trash, even if they do include a few complimentary mints. Keep in mind that property owners who are back due on their taxes will probably be receiving many letters with offers to buy their real estate. These letters come in all different shapes and sizes: formal, informal, handwritten, mass produced, postcards, certified, and anything else someone can think of!

Case Study

After acquiring a property in Deltona, Florida, we entered the premises. The property was in very bad shape, and after inspecting the pigsty that lay beyond the front door, we could see a mountain of mail—and when we say mountain, we are not exaggerating! We cleaned more than 10 tons of garbage out of this property—the owner seemed to have a love for 10-year-old newspapers and empty beer bottles. Among the garbage, we counted 27 pieces of mail consisting of letters, postcards, door notes, and Fed-Ex envelopes, all from companies attempting to purchase the home prior to the Tax Deed sale.

Knock on the Door

We have found this to be the most effective way of speaking to the owners. Your personality and ability to cope with other people's hardships will be the key to having a successful conversation with the owner, as opposed to being chased away from the property by a pack of attack dogs.

You must be prepared for ANY reaction to your introduction. For most of us, it seems unimaginable to face even the possibility that our home might be sold due to non-payment of taxes. Unfortunately for some people, it is a reality.

Imagine working all your life to build a home, family, and future. Unfortunately, you run into hardship in the form of divorce, disability, unemployment, or a death in the family. Imagine how you would feel if someone knocked on your door, offering to purchase your home because of back due real estate taxes. Does this sound like an event you would want to avoid? Keep that in mind when you approach a distressed owner, and really try to help them by offering alternative choices. Even if you can't help them, maybe they will be grateful that they had someone to talk to who understood their situation.

The Un-helpable

There will be times you may not be able to help the owner. Sometimes the owner is upside-down in the property. This means they owe more than the property is worth. In their mind, moving may not be feasible, even though it is inevitable. Other people may refuse help due to pride or sentimental reasons. It is up to you to put forth the offer, but they will have to meet you half-way by accepting your help and choosing your solution. If they choose not to help themselves, you may end up owning their property after the auction! This sounds harsh, but the reality is that if they don't accept some form of help, they may lose their home regardless. Try to think of other creative solutions that may assist them. One such solution is as follows:

Case Study

John owned a home in Orlando, FL, but he had to stop working due to an illness. John's property was due to be auctioned by the County. John was unwilling to negotiate with investors because he did not understand the situation, and he felt pressured to make a huge decision in a short amount of time. Since John owed much less on his mortgage than his property was worth, he received an offer to have his real estate taxes paid off while he still remained the owner. John signed a Promissory Note that gave the investor an option to buy his home within 60 days of when the taxes were paid. If he was able to pay the investor back, plus interest and fees, within the 60 days, John would keep his house, and the investor would receive a handsome return on his investment. If John was unable to pay back the investor within the time frame, the investor would be able to purchase the home at a pre-determined price. This situation gave John an opportunity to search for alternative solutions without such a tight deadline, allowing him to feel less pressured. John was able to secure cheaper living accommodations with a relative, so the investor purchased his home. John was able to pocket a nice profit on his home, while the investor helped him out of a difficult situation that could have resulted in the complete loss of his home. This story was a win-win situation for all. Those are the types of real estate deals we love the most!

Research

Research is the most important part of Tax Deed investing. Poor research leads to poor investments. Research will make or break your investment. Our motto and number one rule for real estate investments (including Tax Deeds) is:

Profit is made when you buy, not when you sell!

We are solid advocates of the simple truth that if you do not purchase the property at the right price, then it will be very difficult to make a profit, unless there are adverse changes in the market. There may be an increase in property values while you own it, but then again, appreciation may also remain flat, or, worse yet, go down. Our company has prided itself on making sure we buy at the right price so that, short of a natural disaster, we can make a profit. We even have a case where we DID have a natural disaster—3 hurricanes, to be exact—and we STILL made money! (We'll explain that story later). Our point is that the tedious research you complete BEFORE the auction will turn you into a savvy investor who is aware of important price points. There may be months where you attend lots of auctions and never purchase a property. Don't give up! Remember, when you do successfully purchase a property, you will be extremely knowledgeable, and will have reduced the risks that exist in the investment.

What is involved in research? To fully research a property, we need to do the following:

1. Locate the property.
2. Evaluate the market trends in the area in which you will purchase.
3. Evaluate the property's worth, both as-is and in peak condition.
4. Estimate our costs of repair, holding, and selling.
5. Evaluate acceptable profit amounts.
6. Evaluate the size and scope and decide if it is within your capabilities.

Let's get started!

Parcel IDs or Alt Key

Most counties use either a parcel ID or an Alt key. This is the equivalent of a social security number for a property. This is how most tax deed records will identify the property.

Example

We'll use Orange County, Florida as our data base. Go to www.ocpafl. org. This is the Property Appraiser's website for Orange County in Florida. There is a button on the left labeled "Record Searches". Most counties have a legal disclaimer attached to the information they provide to the public so as to avoid lawsuits if the information is wrong. The only way to access their data is to agree to the disclaimer. After entering, you will be able to search properties in multiple ways, including Parcel ID, Owner Name, Address, Property Names, Plat Book/Page, etc. Most of the time, we will either use the parcel ID or the owner's name. Using the parcel ID is always the most accurate way to gain information. We always use the parcel ID when researching Tax Deed properties. It is THAT specific parcel which is going up for auction, so that is what we should be researching. The owner may own multiple properties, and we want to be sure we are researching the correct one.

After we locate the property, we may do another search to see if the owner possesses any other real estate. Sometimes we may even check surrounding counties to see if they own a second home or investment property. The owner may be interested in negotiating before the sale for one or all of their properties. They may be living at a different address that may be listed here as well.

While at the Orange County website, type in the following parcel ID:

33-22-29-4595-03-010

This is broken up into Section, Township, Range, Subdivision, Block, and Lot.

You can either enter each section, or enter it all as one number without any dashes where it says "Full Parcel".

The example we used is a property that our company purchased 09/23/2003 for $45,500. We sold it 05/19/2004 for $95,000. This page will give you quite a bit of information.

It gives you the legal description: LAKE MANN ESTATES UNIT NO 2 Y/96 LOT 1 BLK C

Notice that on 09/23/2003 the Deed Code states TD. This means Tax Deed. If you click on TD, it will provide you with a list of codes and their meanings. The most common codes are WD for Warranty Deed and QC for Quit Claim. Your county may have different codes. TX for Tax Deed is also quite common. Familiarize yourself with the codes in your county. After you research a few properties, you will begin to recognize the important codes.

After entering the parcel ID number, we now have a physical address. Most of the county's tax deed documents don't have the physical address. A physical address is used by the Post Office so it can identify a property for mail delivery purposes. The REAL LOCATION of the property is its Legal Description. This is what the government determines is the property to be sold. There may be times where the address and the Legal Address conflict. ALWAYS go by the legal address of record. If this sounds confusing, think of it as using the government's address rather than the Post Office's address for the purposes of identifying the property.

Case Study

In December of 2003, we were attending an auction in Polk County, Florida. Our research indicated that one of the auctioned properties was a ditch. Yes, that's right, a ditch. The interesting thing was that the ditch had an actual physical mailing address. The problem was that this address was for the property next door, which was a $150,000 home! To an inexperienced investor, this was a disaster waiting to happen. We were certain that an inexperienced investor would bid on this property, not knowing the consequences! Sure enough, when the parcel came up for auction, someone placed a minimum bid. Other investors in the room knew someone was about to purchase a worthless piece of real estate. If that wasn't strange enough, ANOTHER person bid against him! This went on until the bidding got up into the tens of thousands. After about 5 minutes of back and forth bidding, we informed the bidders of what they were bidding on. Some people receive pleasure out of watching other people make expensive mistakes. We, on the other hand, prefer to lend a helping hand whenever possible, and take no pleasure in other people's misfortunes. Upon realizing their mistakes, the 2 investors ended their bidding war. Unfortunately, the winner paid the $200 deposit and had 24 hours to come up with the remaining balance. The investor realized his error and decided not to pay the County for the remaining balance. Due to his non-payment, the investor was banned from bidding at future auctions in that county. The property was re-listed a couple months later and 'struck to the applicant'. In this case, the bidder was fortunate enough to only lose $200 and his bidding rights for one year. So the lesson to be learned here is always complete your research!

Remember; always go by the legal description, not the physical address. If you are using the physical address, make sure you VERIFY it with the legal description. This brings us to another rule of ours: **TRUST BUT VERIFY.**

This rule applies to EVERYTHING. Let's return to our previous online research example.

The County's website shows the property as being "improved", meaning there is a structure on the property. It is not vacant. Be aware, though, that a property containing a building that has been demolished may not reflect this information in the public county records.

The record also contains a value summary, but beware, as these numbers are not always accurate. In our opinion, these calculations or evaluations are usually much lower than the actual market value. In Florida, this is called the Just Value. To find an accurate market value of a property, we generally use a 30% rule, which means that we add another 30% to the listed Just Value to get an approximate market value. If the Just Value is $118,000, then our 30% calculation places the market value around $153,400: $118,000 times 1.3 equals $153,400. This is approximate, but it is a good way to get a feel for what the property will sell for. Every area is different, so you will need to do some research to find a calculation that will work for you in your locality. In some areas, if the market is hot and the prices are escalating quickly, we multiply the Just Value by 1.5. We trust the county's information, but we like to VERIFY the information by researching the neighborhood.

You should calculate numbers that make sense for the County you are interested in. Others may not agree with us about our calculations for Orange County, Florida. We recommend you come up with an equation that you feel reflects the true value of the property.

Some of the County's evaluations are not even close to what a property's real value is. There are many possible reasons for this. The best way to combat these odd figures is scouting the area and becoming familiar with the prices for finished products as well as rehabs.

Most counties provide online overhead maps with additional overlays of information. Those overlays may contain aerial photos, 'Just Values' of homes, names, parcel IDs, etc. By looking at the aerial photographs to see what else is in the neighboring area, and by looking at the Just Values, you should formulate an idea of what a property is worth. The more of these you look at, the easier it becomes, and the quicker you will be able to approximate a true market value.

Most of the counties we pursue Tax Deeds in provide two important reports: Sales Analysis and Similar Sales in Subdivision. These reports will provide you with sales prices for homes located in the surrounding area. If these reports are available for your county, review them carefully, as you may be able to see what the neighboring houses sold for most recently. These two free tools will supply you with very accurate valuation tools.

Below are key questions to which you will need to find answers in order to proceed with the acquisition of any property:

1. What kind of deed was it? (Warranty Deed, Quit Claim Deed, Tax Deed, etc.)
2. From whom was the property purchased?
3. How many heated square feet does it have?
4. How many gross square feet does it have?
5. How many baths does it have?
6. How many bedrooms does it have?
7. What year was it built?
8. If there are later additions, what year were the additions built?
9. Is the structure concrete, wood frame, or other construction?
10. Does it have a pool?
11. What is the size of the lot?
12. What are the annual taxes?
13. When was the property last sold?
14. What are the sales prices in the local area?

These are all important questions, most of which can be answered on the Property Appraiser's website.

If you are attempting to do research on a county that does not have a website, you will need to go down to their office to review documents, or gain access to their computerized information. This can actually be an advantage, as some investors won't make the extra effort to do this. That could mean fewer people to bid against, which is great news for you!

GIS MAPS

Most counties have GIS Maps. GIS stands for Geographical Information Systems. These are more detailed maps that can include not only the parcel information, but also information regarding zones, zoning, future land use, property values, recent sales, school districts, public facilities, soil contents, flood zones, and aerial photographs. Please be aware that any aerial photographs you view may not be up to date, so it is important to view the property.

We sometimes use the GIS maps to locate flood zones. Generally, we only use a GIS map if we are looking to purchase raw land. Most of the photos on the GIS sites are digital photos taken via satellite or by plane. Google has even entered this industry by offering aerial photographs of most of the world at www.earth.google.com. It is amazing what information you can find on the internet, if you know where to look.

To find GIS maps for your local area, go to Google and type in "GIS Maps", and enter your city and state. Remember that the first search item returned may not be the right one, so be sure to look through multiple search results. You may also call your local Property Appraiser's office or Comptroller's office to see if they know the site address or phone contact. Most government sites are free, but you may come across third party sites which will charge you for this free information. We rarely pay to access to this type of information because we can usually find it for free from the county, city, or state. Remember that if someone is charging you a fee to access public information, you too can find the same information the way they did—free of charge!

Most of the county websites have links to the GIS maps because they are so highly requested. Some are city websites, so you may need to search for a GIS in a city rather than a county. Sometimes the State itself has GIS maps as well. When getting started, we recommend you categorize all your web links according to city, county, or state. This will help you navigate though all your links easily and efficiently. There is nothing more frustrating then searching for a site you know you have already visited. Bookmark your links as soon as you find a good one; you can always delete the link later, if you change your mind about it.

Depending on where the parcel is located, you may need to search for a city map instead of a county map. Find out whether the parcel is located inside the city limits, or simply in the county. Remember, a parcel is always located in a county; but it is not always located in a city, even though it may say Orlando, Houston, or whatever city you live near. A city mailing address does not always designate a city location.

On a personal note, we love to use GIS maps. When viewing raw land on the GIS, you can get a good idea of the features of the land. What do we mean by land features? Land quality, elevation, and location of water are all examples of land features. You can even see if the neighbors are using their properties to store junk cars in their back yards. Sometimes you can determine whether there are mature trees on the land, whether the land is overgrown, the location of new developments, or the locations of the closest schools and parks. GIS mapping can be very valuable because it truly gives you a 'picture' of the area. You may believe an area you are interested in is occupied by acres of vacant land; the GIS aerial photographs, if current, can show you how vacant the land really is.

Case Study

We recently purchased a property in Ocoee, FL. The parcel was about 2.7 acres. We were looking for GIS maps in Ocoee, and sure enough we found that it was on the border of Ocoee but not in the city of Ocoee. The parcel was located in what is referred to as Unincorporated Orange County. All the maps would have to go through Orange County, rather than through the city of Ocoee. After locating the Orange County GIS maps, we could see there were no other vacant lots in the area. This parcel was going to be a great piece of land to pick up in order to subdivide and sell off the individual lots. We immediately put a contract in with the listing agent for full price, and the seller agreed to our terms. Within a couple days the seller was hoping we would exit out of the deal as he was receiving offers that were $50,000-$75,000 higher than our contract price! The seller had not completed his research before listing the property, which resulted in the seller pricing the property too low and leaving extra profit on the table for us! Had this person known about GIS maps, he may have asked more for the property.

Tax and Public Records

These records can be a good resource when trying to find relatives or an alternative address for the owner of the property. Although we rarely use the public and tax records web site, it is important that you are aware of this information source.

Most counties have a website dedicated to real estate taxes. You can view the owner's tax bill for the current and past year. This may give you an alternative contact address for the owner of a Tax Deed property. We also use the tax record website to locate other family members connected to the property. We achieve this by entering only the owner's last name. Sometimes we are able to find relatives using this technique, and other times we find people who are unrelated to the property. In some situations, other investors have difficulty in locating the owner of a Tax Deed property, so we make the effort to do the extra research to try to locate the owner. Most likely, the other investors have given up at this point, so this is where our company prevails.

Public records can also be a good source of information. Public records refer to the county records where you would go to "record a deed". Recording a deed is where a deed becomes a public document. Public records can also give you an overall view of circumstances attached to the property. You may find bankruptcies, divorces, deaths, births, and almost anything that may change someone's financial and lifestyle circumstances. These are crucial times in a property owner's life, and may severely impact a person's ability to retain real estate. If you are able to contact an owner who has filed for a bankruptcy or a divorce, be sure to approach them in a way that will be non-offensive, and also convey understanding about their situation. These people may be facing periods of hardship, so treat them with the respect they deserve as human beings, and the respect you would want to receive if you were in their situation.

Case Study

In 2004, there was a property in Deltona, Florida that we were considering purchasing. The owner of record was not responding to any of our letters, mail, or correspondence. We viewed the previous year's tax form, and discovered a different address on record. We researched the alternative address and located a different name. As it turns out, the person at the alternative address was the ex-wife of the new owner. She helped us get in contact with the owner. Without the use of public records, we may not have found another way to find the current owner.

Viewing the property

Time is a precious commodity, and we wish we had more hours in a day. The more properties you look at, the more time it takes. You will eventually become more efficient at choosing which properties to physically look at, and which ones to research online. You have to make decisions about which properties to focus your time and efforts on. There may be 100 Tax Deed properties for sale in one week. Most people do not have time to view them all, and therefore have to be selective.

One of the biggest obstacles we face is the amount of driving time required to physically look at the properties we are interested in. When we began investing in real estate, we would print out the following for each property:

- opening bid amounts
- approximate market value
- GIS maps
- driving directions
- other notes

This was a lot of information and a big waste of paper. In the past, we found something as simple as finding the property a headache, especially if we had 15 properties to view in one day. We weren't sure which property to view in which order, and most of the time we were driving hundreds of needless extra miles because of this. Then one day, we discovered a great website that helped alleviate this problem, and now we have streamlined our property searches.

The website is www.maps.com and we still use it religiously to this day. The annual subscription, in our opinion, is inexpensive and priceless. The most impressive feature of this website is the intelligent mapping system. If you have 10 properties you need to look at, instead of printing 10 maps and trying to decide which order to proceed, you can type in all the property addresses, and maps.com will automatically provide you with the best directions and property viewing order! What a blessing!

We use this site anytime we need to travel to unfamiliar or multiple locations. Even when we are familiar with the neighborhoods, if we have multiple properties, the tools maps.com provides are priceless. They save us hours of driving time and alleviate the frustrations of locating the correct properties in order.

One very helpful tip we can give you is do not physically view properties on your auction list too early. When we began in the Tax Deed business, we viewed upcoming auction properties a week in advance, only to find that most of the properties would be redeemed or removed from the auction. This meant we were wasting tens of hours a week viewing properties that would never be auctioned. Nowadays we try to view the properties no sooner than one day in advance of the auction date. We have found this a huge timesaver, and we strongly recommend you use this approach once you have been successful in purchasing a couple properties and you feel comfortable with your research. When starting out, we recommend viewing properties no more than 3 days in advance of the auction date.

If you do not have a physical address for the property, you will need to be creative. We always have access to the county and city maps through a laptop computer with a wireless broadband connection. These maps are generally public information that do not require fees for usage and are mostly available online. There are many times we have scouted for a vacant parcel which had no address. The solution to locating these properties was to view the aerial photographs on the Property Appraiser's website to locate the land.

To get a location or nearby intersection, we may need to consult a survey or plat map, or understand legal descriptions so we can find an intersection or aerial view that will show us the nearby cross streets. Using those cross streets, we can now find the location.

* WARNING! *

Now, before you delve into this section, we must warn you: we had as much fun writing this as you will have reading it. How much fun?... Absolutely no fun at all. This next section is not required reading, but we felt obligated to include it—more as a reference for the one time you have trouble locating a hard to find piece of land. If you aren't in the mood for some heavy reading, feel free to skip this section and return to it at a later date. Let's see different examples of how we can locate those troublesome properties.

Recorded Plat Survey

Almost all properties have a parcel ID that is broken up into Section, Township, Range, Subdivision, Block and Lot. This is called a recorded plat survey. Some counties do not use a parcel ID; they use a "folio number" or an "Alt Key".

Most counties use this system of recorded plats. It is created by the developer, who is building in the area or who is putting in the infrastructure on the land. A surveyor would go out to the parcel of land, locate the boundaries, and plat it. Then, guided by the zoning requirements, he can subdivide the parcel into smaller parcels; make roadways, drainage, and easements, and so forth. The finished plat is then recorded with the county, making easy reference for the person or company reselling the individual lots. Plats can be amended, changed, combined, and/or further subdivided.

Example

Orange County Florida: 33-22-29-4595-03-010
This parcel ID is interpreted into the following information:
Section 33, Township 22, Range 29, Subdivision 4595, Block 03, Lot 010

We could just type this into the Orange County Property Appraiser's website. But what would we do if we didn't have access to a website? What if we only had access to a printed map on record at the county records department? How do we view this information for the property being auctioned?

We could go to the county records department and ask for the correct map, based on this information. Each of these numbers and labels has a specific function. Since this subdivision is recorded, we can ask for the map that includes this subdivision. The map could be one page or it could be hundreds of pages. The subdivision is further broken up into blocks that are usually separated by streets. The blocks are broken up into lots which are usually numbered in order. If you are looking for Block 03 and you see a map of Block 05, you know that you are close and Block 5 is probably on an adjoining map. The block we are using in our example is 03 and the lot is 010. This is seen as 03010 and it is highlighted.

Most maps separate these two numbers of blocks and lots. They may have the number 3 within a circle. This would represent the block number. The individual lots are then numbered. If you need to view a map and have difficulty in locating the parcel, ask the person who provided you with the map. They are generally happy to help. Be patient with the county record employees, as there is a lot you can learn from them. This is their job, and generally we find they are a BIG source of information. Maybe the employee has had other requests for the map you are requesting. Maybe the person requesting the map gave the employee some insider information regarding the area. Information is the key in real estate, and every person you come in contact with can help you paint a picture regarding whether a property is a worthwhile investment or just a waste of time.

Metes and Bounds Survey

The Metes and Bounds survey system is the oldest and most direct method for describing land. To survey by metes and bounds, a surveyor describes the boundaries of the property by stating the distance and direction from one corner of the property to the next. A simple example of a metes and bounds legal description is as follows:

"Starting at the southeast corner of ABC property, then due south for 100' to the point of beginning, then due east for 200', then due south 200', then due west 200', then due north 200'." This describes a square parcel of land which is 200 feet on each side.

Government Rectangular Survey

These government surveys form the base from which all subsequent private surveys are made.

In 1785, Congress passed the first law for surveying the new territories of the United States. The initial part of the wilderness to be surveyed was the eastern portion of what is now known as Ohio. As each new area was surveyed, the first task was to select a beginning point. In Oregon, this point is called the Willamette Stone, located near downtown Portland. After the beginning point was selected, a principal meridian (or line) was surveyed straight North and South through the beginning point. There are 31 such Principal Meridians throughout the United States, each with a unique name. In Oregon, it is called the Willamette Meridian.

An East-West line, called the baseline, was also surveyed through the beginning point for each territory surveyed. The baselines and meridians are further broken down by lines stretching North-South and East-West, at intervals of six miles each. These lines create squares which are six miles on each side. These "thirty six square mile" squares are called Townships. Townships are referred to by their distance North or South of the baseline and their distance East or West of the meridian. The numbering to the North starts at T1N (read "township one North"). To the South, the number starts with T1S (read "township one South").

The Range is a specific vertical row. There can be Eastern Ranges and Western Ranges, depending on the state. If your state has both, the legal should have an extra letter such as R18E or R18W. The R stands for Range, E for East, and W for West.

The Township is a horizontal row. There can be Northern Townships and Southern Townships, depending on the state. If your state has both, the legal should have an extra letter such as T32N or T32S. The T stands for Township, N for North, and S for South.

These two coordinates will meet at a point similar to an XY axis. This point consists of a six mile by six mile block. Each 36 square mile parcel identified by a township and range number is further divided into 36 SECTIONS, where each section is theoretically 1 square mile, or 640 acres. The cells are numbered "boustrophedonically", or "as the cow plows", which means that the numbers wrap around in an "S" shape. Such a numbering system was easier for surveyors to use when they were doing the original survey.

Many parcels of land are smaller than an entire section. They sometimes are the size of a *quarter section*. Each section is divided into 4 quarters, each 1/4 square mile, or 160 acres. Each of the quarter sections is labeled with a quadrant direction. In our example, the description is referring to the Southwest quarter section of section 24, which is in white. Again, be sure to read the description from back to front so you know which quarter section the description is referring to.

Quarter sections can be further divided into 4 more parts (called the *quarter-quarter section*), each 1320 feet in length, or 1/4 of a mile, which results in 1,742,400 square feet, or 40 acres.

Finally, we have the quarter section that can also be further divided into halves and so forth.

We told you in the beginning, this area of real estate can be quite boring...Let's forage forward!

Putting it all together

Now you have multiple ways of locating the property. Through understanding these maps, you can now locate a property that may otherwise be difficult to find. By locating the property, we can now look around the area, find the closest intersecting street, and drive to see the property.

Too many investors purchase land sight unseen. We do not recommend this. Have we done it? Yes, but only twice. Both times, it caused unnecessary stress, and we worried profusely until we viewed the property.

Make sound investments by FULLY researching the property; view it with your own eyes.

CHAPTER 3

In this chapter, you will learn:

- How to evaluate a property: Is it a good deal?
- How to use Realtors and the MLS
- How to estimate repair costs
- Tips for dealing with contractors
- How to estimate holding, selling costs, and actual profit

Evaluating a Property

These next sections will contain less detail because we want to focus on the Tax Deed acquisition process rather than the basics of general real estate investing. You will need to investigate these topics more thoroughly.

There are many sources you can pool together to get an approximate value of a property. Here are some of the sources we use:

Realtors and MLS

The best way to value a property is by looking at comparable sales, or "comps", as the real estate industry more commonly calls them. Comps are the prices which similar properties have sold for; properties which are located in the same geographical area as the property you are interested in. We are fortunate enough to have realtor friends who provide us with comps whenever we need them. As you start out, you may not have this luxury. I urge you to find a friend, relative, or associate who has access to the MLS "Multiple Listing Service". This is where most of the properties for sale will be listed. Not only is it a current list, it will have all the pending contracts and past sales. This information is near priceless.

We use our relationships with realtors in the exchange of information and research. These realtors don't mind putting in a little work when they know they will receive our listing when we are ready to sell the property. We have even SOLD a property to one of our realtors! These relationships can prove to be invaluable. Most will operate on an "I'll scratch your back if you'll scratch mine" basis. Scratch away! You can also ask for a commission discount on your listing when you sell your investment property.

Technically speaking, realtors are not allowed by law to give you access to MLS. Only licensed brokers, salespeople, appraisers, and inspectors are supposed to have access. Our advice is to FIND ACCESS. If you find this information to be as valuable as we do, it may be in your best interest to get a real estate license, an appraisal license, or an inspector license so you gain your own access to the MLS.

MLS can help you pin-point what properties are selling for per square foot, locate sales within school districts, visualize trends in prices, and potentially see pictures of properties.

Most realtors will charge between 2.5%- 3.5% commissions per side of a sales transaction. If you keep all your business with one realtor, he or she may be willing to reduce their commission fees. We have some realtors that will reduce their commission down to 1% on the listing side. That can save you a lot of money! That is an extra $2,000 in our pocket per $100,000 of the sales price. A $300,000 sales transaction nets us an extra $6,000!

Why would our realtor reduce his commission for us? Our company comes across at least 3-7 deals a week. Some deals are gold, though most are fools gold; so out of all the deals that our sources present to us, we may only aggressively pursue 1 or 2 deals a month. The deals we don't pursue are researched and presented to our friends and business associates so they can then evaluate the properties for their own use.

We complete some of the due diligence needed before we hand the deal to another group or person, and the people we present these deals to really appreciate the extra research we do! Why would we want to hand real estate deals to other investors? We gladly hand out deals to our business contacts for multiple reasons:

The more they make, the more we make

If my realtor makes $30,000 on a deal, do you think he might give us a referral incentive? Absolutely. He is happy to give a referral because without us, there would have been no deal.

Don't be greedy, share the wealth

The more deals you pursue and complete, the more you will realize just how many deals there are out there. Some deals may be unaffordable for your pocketbook, so you may need to partner up with another investor or simply hand them over to another person in exchange for a finder's fee. If you are doing business with the right people, they will gladly do the same for you.

Shared interest in the same markets

Let's imagine you are evaluating a property, and you crunch the numbers and decide the deal is not profitable enough for the amount of involvement and risk. Now you decide to turn the deal over to a business associate and inform them of the numbers you have calculated. After they look at your numbers, they present you with new information showing that the area in which the deal is located could justify higher values. Perhaps a new development that you didn't know about is under construction nearby. Maybe a new law in the works that will change the zoning laws in the area could benefit this property. Your shared interest in the same market INCREASES your information and ability to compute whether it is a good deal or not.

Case Study

In late 2005, we held a contract on a property that had a defect in the existing survey. We needed to close on the property within a 2 week time period or we would lose the $43,000 deposit securing the property. The seller was anxious to terminate our contract, and would not extend our closing date because he had received several back-up cash offers which were in excess of our original contract price. He wanted our contract to fall through so he could keep the $43,000 and accept a higher priced back-up contract. Unfortunately, our survey company could not complete the boundary survey within the required time period. Luckily, through our realtor's good contacts, we located someone who was willing to put us in front of their existing customers, so we were saved. This can happen in any area of real estate: architectural, engineering, appraisal, etc. Realtors deal with these types of industry people on a daily basis. Network and use your professional contacts so you have a list of possibilities when you need them.

If you are fortunate enough to gain access to MLS or a similar service, you will be able to use certain tools and search by area, map, street, and so forth to value a property. We usually use the mapping feature to select any properties around our target property. We will read through the descriptions to see whether the property is in good condition or in need of repairs.

The MLS allows you to see how long the property was on the market. Was it 2 days, 2 months, or 2 years? We have seen properties sit on the MLS for well over a year; it is our job to figure out why such a property isn't quick to sell. A basic understanding of the time frame needed to sell a property can be the difference between a grand slam deal and money loser. Be aware of your market conditions and how they change on a weekly, monthly, and annual basis.

There are many reasons why a property does not sell within a reasonable amount of time. Here are some reasons:

- The location is poor
- Real estate market is flat—supply exceeds demand
- Local or national economy is weak
- Interest rates are high
- Property is in need of repairs
- Awkward floor plan
- Mold issues exist
- The neighbors store half-built cars in their driveway
- The homeowner may have unfriendly pets
- The seller's realtor may be difficult to contact
- The seller may be difficult to contact
- There may be termite issues
- Code violations may exist
- Liens exist on the property
- The seller may be asking more than market value, resulting in appraisal problems
- The property may have settling and/or title issues

There are so many possibilities that we can't list them all.

Conversely, a property can sell very quickly. Here are some reasons why a property would sell quickly:

- The area of town is undergoing redevelopment by investors or real estate developers.
- The property is in disrepair and is priced accordingly.
- The homeowner created a great marketing plan and provided a pleasant atmosphere to potential buyers.
- Demand exceeds supply creating a fast moving market
- The realtor created a brochure highlighting all the extra features of the property that weren't obvious to traditional buyers.

- The seller may have given their realtor the ability to accept or deny contracts on their behalf.
- The seller provided useful information such as inspections or appraisals. A potential buyer would be happy to have these reports provided to them. This is considered going above and beyond.
- The seller may be asking for an asking price below current market price.

Again, we cannot list all the possibilities, but these should give you a good starting point for consideration.

Drive by the Property

When we are looking to purchase a property, not only do we like to view the MLS listings, we also like to do a drive-by of the neighborhood where the property is located. This way, we can actually see which houses sold for which dollar amount. After you complete four or five of these drive-bys, you should be able to make quicker analysis of the neighborhoods. Remember that neighborhoods can vary from street to street. This is especially true in the high end neighborhoods. Many times we have seen $750,000 to $1 million homes located next to a home valued at less than $200,000. The difference in values may be attributed to something such as a gated street. When a property is located in a gated community, this can drastically increase its value. The ability to correctly value property is an essential skill in being successful at purchasing Tax Deed properties.

Don't underestimate the importance of viewing a property in which you are interested. As a beginner, we highly recommend you drive by every property you are interested in. This may be frustrating at times, because you will see MANY properties without purchasing a single one, so you must think of this as your real estate education. Each time you view a property, you are learning about the neighborhoods, what the houses are worth, and the type of people who live in the area.

In the beginning, we disliked driving around all day looking at properties we may or may not be successful in acquiring. As time passed, we discovered the main benefit of viewing these properties: they enabled us to learn about all the local areas and how the property values were determined. This information has proven to be valuable, because now, when the auction properties are listed, our research time is cut down considerably, as we are extremely knowledgeable about property locations.

For some properties, we can look at just the zip codes and write them off as poor investments, or flag them as good investments, because we know the areas so well. We are more aware of which areas are selling for what dollar amounts. We know which areas are developing and which are declining, as well as which investors are interested in which geographical areas!

It is helpful to take notes on the surrounding properties in an area you are researching. Are there any for sale signs in front yards? If so, call and find out how much the property is selling for and what the square footage is! See how easy it is to find a comp? If a realtor answers the phone when you call, ask if they have anything else for sale in the same neighborhood. When dealing with these realtors, be sure not to take advantage of their services. At some point, you may actually deal with that person, and you don't want to be remembered as the person who asked a million questions and never purchased anything. Ask what you need and end the phone call.

Online Auctions

Non-traditional sources of information can sometimes be the most informative. EBay and other online auction sites list thousands of properties just about anywhere in the world. We have even seen groups advertising Tax Deeded properties they purchased in their county!

Guess what? We are one of them. In fact, we SOLD a Tax Deed property we owned on EBay for a 400% profit! Read the details in our Stories Section!

Be aware that most of the asking prices will be at least market price or more, but there are some rare deals to be found. Most of the sellers ask too much, as they are usually inexperienced or unknowledgeable. You may ask: why is a website such as EBay a good source for real estate? If you monitor these websites often enough, you will find the selling price of properties in your city, providing you with an additional source for comps. These sales will give you a good idea of what the highest and lowest market prices are. If there are bids on the property, there is a chance it was priced fairly.

Case Study

A developer in Orlando built 4 town homes in downtown Orlando in 2006. He had previously sold 3 of the units, and decided to list the forth unit on EBay to see what price he could achieve. He listed the property using a 60 day auction. We valued the unit at approximately

$325,000 (market value). We personally placed a bid of $100,000. We knew the chances of winning the auction at that price were slim, but we have seen stranger things happen. By the end of the auction, the property sold for $300,100.00 plus a 5% bidder's fee. This was actually a fair price for this property. In our opinion, it was a little below market price. There were other fees added on that brought the total cost very close to the $325,000.00 price. This auction only reaffirmed our opinion of what properties were selling for in that area of downtown Orlando.

There are some smaller online auction sites that are hired by banks and attorneys to sell their foreclosure and estate properties. We like to keep an eye on these auctions. Even if we have no intention purchasing the properties, the results can be a good indicator of market values for specific neighborhoods.

Just Values and Public Records

Another tool for evaluating market values for real estate is "Just Values". These numbers are the local county's "market value". These terms can be confusing and misleading. We do not use Just Values as true market values. We use Just Values to approximate what we believe the market values of properties are.

Example

Let's say we find a property of interest in Orlando, Florida. Next, we look at the map on the Orange County Property Appraiser's website, as this website allows us to overlay the Just Values on the overhead map for all the houses located in a certain area. Let's assume we see a range of Just Values from $220k-$240k. After viewing the details of five or six recently sold properties, we find most of these were in the region of 2000 heated square feet. Our target property is 2000 square feet, the same size as these recently sold properties. We do not look at the gross square footage; we only look at the heated square footage, since sales prices are calculated in this manner. We see that, on average, the comparable properties were selling for $300k. The just value of the target property is $240k.

If we divide $300,000 by $240,000, the result is 1.25. This number becomes our multiplier. We generally use a multiplier of 1.25 to 1.3. So, if we see a just value of $200k, we multiply that by 1.25 to get a value of $240,000 for that property. These numbers are never exact, but it gives us a good valuation range.

Along with the Just Values, we can do some simple math. Let's say we look at the sales history in the neighborhood and see sales of 5 properties in the last year. Each of these properties were 2000 heated sq ft and sold for $300,000. Using this number, we can calculate the cost per square foot. So, simply put, it is $300,000 divided by 2000 heated square feet, which equals $150 per square foot. Now, if we have a property that is 2200 heated square feet, we can calculate $150 X 2200 = $330,000. Remember, this is never an exact number, but more of a guide. It will be up to you and the end to determine exactly what the property is worth.

Most books will recommend that you purchase an appraisal for every property you buy. Time constraints and cost issues have led us to avoid purchasing appraisals for Tax Deed properties. Since you will not have access to the interior of the property before you purchase, this will make an appraisal difficult. Please understand that we aren't telling you **not** to order an appraisal. If this will make you more comfortable, then, by all means, order one. The appraiser will not be able to do a complete appraisal without gaining access to the inside of the property. The problem is, if you order appraisals for 50 properties and end up purchasing only one, you will have spent tens of thousands of wasted dollars. You will need to use your valuation and research experience as well as your gut feelings.

Estimating Repair Costs

Many books have been written on estimating repair costs, and we have read most of them. Again, our main purpose in this book is to familiarize you with the Tax Deeds process. We can almost guarantee you will have to perform some repairs to a property you buy at a Tax Deed auction. Some items may be small, such as replacing a window or painting; others may be larger, such as replacing a roof or remodeling a kitchen.

When we started our real estate business, we weren't very familiar with estimating repair costs. So in order to become more familiar with repair costs, we spent several hours wandering the aisles of Home Depot pricing common materials. Items we priced included exterior doors, interior doors, windows, carpet, tile, paint and equipment, plants, toilets, sinks, fixtures, and ceiling fans.

Now, obviously, this is not a complete list; but we urge you to become familiar with these item costs, and the time needed to install these items. You may come up with two different figures here: the cost of hiring a contractor to do the work, or the cost of hiring yourself to do the work. Sometimes you can do simple item installations yourself, such as ceiling fans and light fixtures. This will save you money in the long run so long as you don't mind learning a few simple techniques. The main technique for you to learn is reading the item's installation instructions. However, more complicated repairs are best left to the professionals, such as roofing, plumbing, concrete, and termite removal.

If you decide to attempt the work yourself, we recommend you partner with someone who is knowledgeable about repairs or construction. Working with such a person will increase your knowledge regarding material and labor costs. Some people despise the idea of performing repairs while others live for it. You may find you enjoy completing some of the work. The benefit of completing repair work yourself is cost savings, and the ability to accurately assess repair costs for future projects. The more properties you complete, the more informed you will become; this knowledge will prevent you from being taken advantage of when you do decide to hire contractors to complete repair jobs. Next time a contractor quotes you $5000 to paint a house, you will know that the paint only costs $500 and the time involved is only 3 days.

Nowadays, we can drive by a property, look inside, walk the perimeter, and assess the repair costs within 5 or 10 minutes. Are we always correct? Not often, but we are usually close! It is always a little more or a little less, but we are usually within a 10% range.

It is our responsibility to control costs through deciding what "needs" to be repaired and what we would "like" to repair. These two deciding factors can punish your budget and profit margins. Human nature leads us to become emotionally attached to real estate. More often than not, amateur real estate investors walk into properties thinking, "I wouldn't live here unless it had this feature and that feature".

Think about this:

Next time you are driving down the interstate, take note of the houses that either face or back up to the interstate. Personally, we look at these houses and wonder why on earth anyone would want to live next to all that noise and pollution. Now take note of how many of these houses look occupied. Most of the time, you will find they are all occupied, which means someone purchased these houses. The point is that there is always a buyer for almost every piece of real estate, no matter what the circumstances are, so long as the price is fair.

For this very reason, it is very important to emotionally detach yourself from any project you are working on. Make sure you present a good product; we NEVER recommend using sub-grade materials. You must decide which quality of products fit the neighborhood and price range your property is located in. It is no good installing granite countertops into a condo that will retail for $50,000. Nor is it advisable using Formica countertops in a $1 million home.

Make sure you become familiar with the existing products in your neighborhood, and try to steer along the same lines. You don't want to be the cheapest or the most expensive house in the neighborhood.

Here are some main points to consider when doing your repairs and hiring contractors:

Make sure to get multiple bids, and remember that the lowest bid is not always the best. Always get the bids in writing.

Many times when choosing a contractor in the past, we have accepted the highest or middle bid because we knew they could complete the job on time and on budget. Sometimes there is a reason the contractor is the lowest bidder, and this can be seen in their quality of work or responsiveness to your telephone calls. Always get the bids in writing, and make sure the contractor writes down the full scope of the job.

Always keep change orders to a minimum and make sure they are provided in writing.

Sometimes you will need to change the scope of work during the remodeling process. Always make sure you authorize work order changes prior to the completion of the work, and make sure these changes are given to the contractor and signed off! We cannot stress how important this is, as, if there are any discrepancies later down the road; you will have something in writing to refer to. This will also prevent a contractor from changing the price on you halfway through the job. Small work order changes can amount to big expenses and cause big delays, so make sure you keep your changes to a minimum.

Check the (sub) contractor's references and ask about warrantees.

We hear too many times of investors who get the references and don't call to check on them. If you aren't going to check the references, then why ask for them in the first place? You will be amazed what the references will tell you. Sometimes the references don't even exist, or they are the contractor's friends posing as past customers! That will set off warning bells immediately. A dishonest contractor is the last person you want to hire. If a contractor cannot supply you with a reference list, we recommend finding someone else.

Use the Better Business Bureau or other reputable source to find contractors.

The Better Business Bureau was created to protect consumers and inform them of reputable (and disreputable) businesses. They are there for a reason, and we find it is wise to pick a company that is in good standing with the Bureau. Visit www.bbb.org for more information on how to find your local BBB. We also like to use the website www. angieslist.com. This site has lists of contractors that people have used and left comments on. These customer reviews can be a great start to discovering which contractors you may want to hire and which ones you want to stay clear of. You can always check your local newspapers for contractors who advertise many different services from plumbing to garbage removal. We prefer to hire contractors who have been referred to us from other business associates but in time when this isn't possible we look in the local newspaper such as "The Pennysaver" or search the internet.

View and make a copy of their insurance policy and their license.

We have come in contact with many companies and individuals who claim they are licensed and insured. Nowadays, it takes very little to establish a plumbing or roofing company, and there are many fly-by-night companies that let their insurance expire or never even acquire it in the first place. Make sure the contractors you hire are covered by an adequate insurance policy. Just being bonded is not adequate. They should also be carrying workman's compensation.

Try to see their finished work.

If the contractor works in your area, you should be able to see some of the projects they have completed. If you hire a roofer, go look at a roof that your contractor is in the process of completing or has recently completed. Even if you don't know the first thing about roofing, you may notice other things. You may find people drinking on the job, or find garbage littered everywhere on the jobsite. You may even find an owner willing to talk to you. If you are hiring flooring contractors, viewing past jobs will allow you to see the finished quality. A contractor who takes pride in his work will be more than happy to show you his past projects. Be wary of contractors who are reluctant to do this.

Negotiate the smallest deposit on your contract.

Most contractors will require a deposit to begin work. This is fair enough, but make sure the deposit amount is just that—fair. We have taken bids from contractors who asked for a 50% deposit. One contractor even asked to be paid in full for the job before he would begin work. We recommend you never give a contractor more than a 10% deposit. Sometimes you will need to be flexible with the contractor's request. If the contractor owns a small business and you need him to purchase a $30,000 gold bathtub, you may need to provide a larger deposit for this item. Generally a 10% deposit is sufficient. Our target is 10% to 25% as a maximum. If the contractor is reputable, he really shouldn't need your deposit financially to begin the work. In one case, a contractor we hired was using our deposit money to finish work at another jobsite. Be very wary if a contractor approaches you for more money after you have provided him with a deposit.

Case Study

A friend of ours named David decided to remodel his master bathroom. The materials he chose were extremely high-end and quite costly, and the entire bathroom remodel was quoted at $40,000 by the contractor. Feeling quite comfortable with the contractor he chose, David received the quote in writing and was then asked for a deposit of $20,000. When asked why the deposit amount was so much, the contractor explained that he needed to pay for all the materials in advance and needed a bigger deposit from David in order to do this. Without too much thought, David handed the contractor a check for $20,000. Nine days later, David tried calling the contractor to find out why the work on his master bathroom had not begun, only to be greeted by a voicemail. Two days later, this voicemail turned into a disconnected number recording. Two weeks later, David discovered the contractor had filed bankruptcy. His $20,000 was never recovered. Obviously, this looks like fraud because it was later obvious that this contractor had no intention of completing the job. Although such blatant fraud is rare, it clearly illustrates the extreme end of what could possibly go wrong if you aren't careful. You should always use caution when hiring a contractor. ALWAYS check references. If David had checked the contractor's references, this situation could have been avoided.

If you hire a General Contractor, be aware of how much work is subcontracted out to other companies.

This is a tricky subject. Most General Contractors (or GC's) make a minimum of 20% profit (some make up to 100%). Make sure you ask the GC if the people working on your project work directly for him or if he is subcontracting the work to other companies. If all the work is going to be subcontracted out, then why do you need him? The GC is going to collect a (large) fee for handing out all the work to other people! Most GC's have a crew that completes the majority of the work. After this work is completed, the GC may decide to subcontract out any remaining work. Be aware of who is completing each piece of work. Some people view the purpose of hiring a GC as eliminating the headaches of hiring many different people to complete many different repairs, and these people don't mind paying the extra fees for this convenience. That attitude is okay for a residential homeowner, but not for you. These extra GC fees can mean the difference between making a profit and losing money on an entire project, so we personally would rather find the subcontractors ourselves and increase our profit margins.

Calculate out how much contractors are making per hour and make sure it is fair.

Most tradesmen charge between $25 and $75 an hour. This is for skilled trades.

Case Study

In March 2004, we received a bid from Bill, the painting contractor, for $3000. The job was to paint the exterior of a 2200 square foot single-story home. He told us he would need 20 gallons of paint to complete the job. In 2004, good quality paint was about $100 for a 5 gallon bucket or $400 for 20 gallons of paint. Bill explained he would have a helper. When asked how long it would take to complete, Bill estimated 2 days. We calculated that if Bill and his helper finished the job working 8 hours a day for 2 days, he would be making $162.50 per hour! ($2600 divided by 16). Even if he paid his helper $200 a day, his income will still be $2200. Oh no, Bill's down to $137.50 per hour! Does that sound high to you? We truly do believe in paying our employees fairly. When people make good money, they stay happy and loyal. We explained to Bill that even our attorney doesn't make $137.50 per hour and he spent $100,000 on law school! We proceeded to offer Bill $50 per hour times 16 hours plus paint plus $400 for his help. That totaled $1600, which we believed was more than fair. Bill thought otherwise and grumbled under his breath as he walked away, but accepted the job anyways. Contractors will always bid high so remember that, similar to car buying, everything is negotiable, and it is your job to figure out these costs for your project.

Get a written contract without complicated legal language.

Make the contract as simple as possible. Complicated legal mumbo jumbo can land you in a world of hurt in a courtroom. A simple sheet of paper with the dollar amount, completion items, and contact information for all parties are all you need. Make the agreement quick, easy to read, signed and dated, and to the point.

Make sure you have a final deadline date, deadlines for progress, and include penalties for delays.

If the project has staged payments, make sure you have a "start date" by which all other dates are measured. We like to make sure our contracts state "calendar days" rather than business days. This way, the contractor can't fight you by saying he agreed to "work days", a phrase which means Monday through Friday excluding legal holidays. This can delay you MANY weeks. The contract should have a final date ALL the work is to be completed. Too many times in our early investment days, we began a project only to find out we were being taken advantage of. There was always a sob story, so you must be firm or you will be taken advantage of. Penalties must be put in place if the contractor is unable to complete the work by the date agreed upon. We make this date firm but fair. We suggest a penalty fee of between $50 and $150 a day, depending on the scope of the work. If your fee is fair, the contractor should agree to it. If a contractor does not agree to a contract with time delay penalties, that may be a good indicator that he won't finish your project on time.

Make sure the contractors pull all necessary permits.

Many investors will disagree with this, but if you are determined to resell the house, we seriously recommend it. There are some jobs, such as re-roofing, that we will not allow the contractor to start work until we see proof a permit was pulled. If they didn't pull the permit, there is probably a reason. Maybe they don't have insurance or are in trouble with the county. Some smaller items (depending on your county) are often done without permits, even though they are required. These items can be windows, water heaters, etc. Again, we recommend pulling the permit, even though these repair items seem easy. If you don't pull a permit and get caught, the fines can be hefty; and, worst of all, you can receive the dreaded Stop Work Order from the local Code Enforcement Inspector.

Agree to a waiver of lien at each stage.

Again, if the job is lengthy, there should be stages in which the contractor is paid. You want to cover yourself by making sure the General Contractor pays his subcontractors, and by insisting on a written waiver of lien, so that the General Contractor's subcontractors can only place a lien on him, not on your property. If a subcontractor were to place a lien on your property, this would prevent you from selling it because the title would not be clean. We recommend you consult an attorney concerning this issue before hiring any work on your property, so you fully understand the ramifications of lien waivers.

Case Study

Our company renovated 6 condo conversions in which we hired a general contractor to complete the work. Renovations included the installation of new granite countertops for all the kitchens. We experienced severe delays with the general contractor to the point where our contract was re-written three times imposing steeper and steeper financial delay penalties. Finally, after 5 months, the work was completed and the general contractor was paid. Once the units were placed on the market for sale, we received a call from the granite company inquiring about payment! We REQUIRED a lien release from all subcontractors, including the granite company, before we paid the general contractor in full; but, unfortunately, we overlooked the granite company's lien release. Fortunately, we had an ironclad agreement with our general contractor that showed he was responsible for paying all the subcontractors bills, including the granite company. We could have had serious consequences from overlooking this lien release. We provided all the paperwork to the granite company, and they pursued the general contractor for payment. If the granite company had not been so understanding, they could have sued us and attempted to attach a lien to our property due to non-payment,. This would have caused MAJOR problems when we tried to sell the property. The lesson here is always make sure you get lien releases from each contractor that completes work for you.

Insist on a 20% punch list and holdback.

A punch list is created prior to a contractor's final walkthrough on a property. This is an opportunity for the property owner to list all the small problems that are overlooked during construction and remodeling. A holdback is an amount of money that is held back from the final payment to ensure that all the work is completed to the property owner's satisfaction. Most contractors do not implement a holdback. If they do have a holdback, it is usually only 10%. Cover yourself from poor craftsmanship: attempt to get 20% holdback, or as close to it as possible. It is of no benefit for a contractor to allow a holdback amount. Once the work is completed on your project, the last thing contractors wants to do is to return to your jobsite to fix the problems they missed. A good holdback amount is something you must always insist on.

Example

If your total rehab is $5000, then you should implement a holdback amount of 10%—20% in order to make sure ALL the work is completed to an acceptable standard. The holdback means that when the contractor has completed your project, he receives all his payment minus $500—$1000 of the total price. This amount is held back until you walk through the property and verify that ALL the work has been satisfactorily completed. Maybe some of the corners need to be touched up, or a leaky faucet needs to be fixed. Maybe some of the tiles were installed incorrectly, or someone forgot to caulk the tub or windows. There are so many little items that can be missed. For that reason, it is wise to hold back AT LEAST 10%.

If you cannot get the contractor to return to finish the job, you can use this holdback amount to hire someone else. We always try to negotiate a 20% holdback, just in case the contractor provides us with less than perfect workmanship. Remember, if the contractor has no holdback amount to collect, he will have no reason to want to return to your jobsite to complete the work. Money is the main motivation for most contractors!

Estimated Holding and Selling Costs

Have you noticed how many television shows there are documenting the exploits of people buying and selling houses? We love these shows but the one thing that concerns us the most is the amount of profit these shows are portraying the investors make on each deal. Sometimes these projected numbers maybe be correct but sometimes the number don't tell a realistic story about costs involved on buying and selling real estate. We just want you to be aware of the following:

Let's look at a simple deal:

Property Purchase Price:	$150,000
Repair Cost:	$15,000
Sales Price:	$200,000
Profit:	$35,000

How many times have you seen an equation like this? This is the equation that some real estate books and television shows use. It is too simplified to always be totally "true". The realistic numbers probably look something like this:

Property Purchase Price:	$150,000
Repair Cost:	$15,000
Insurance:	$1,000
Title Clearing and Closing Costs:	$2,500
Realtor Fees:	$6,000
Interest:	$6,000
Sales Price:	$200,000
Profit:	$19,500

There is significant difference between $35,000 and $19,500 in profit. Let's be realistic about those numbers. We aren't saying you can't make $35,000 from an investment of $150,000, as it is possible to make much more. Just be aware that there are more costs involved than just repairs.

What if we were splitting the profit with a partner? Now our profit per person is below $10,000! Don't forget Uncle Sam the taxman! There goes another 15%—45%, depending on your tax bracket! We aren't telling you this to discourage you, but we want you to be realistic when calculating your profit margins.

Always make sure you insure any property you purchase. This should be one of the first tasks you complete. If you don't acquire the correct insurance, you are taking dangerous risks. Insurance is cheap, and, at some point, you will need to purchase it. If you don't have insurance, you run the risk of being sued, or having your home swept away by a hurricane, tornado, or flood and not receiving any compensation for your horrendous loss.

Tax Deeds require special attention to Title Clearing, since all Tax Deeds do not come with a clear title. There are fees associated with clearing clouded titles which we will discuss in detail later in the book.

When you sell your property, you can use the For Sale by Owner or "FSBO" method. Realtors will always advise you against selling your property using the FSBO method. We would go so far as to say realtors hate the FSBO method. Why? If every person used FSBO to sell their homes, realtors would be out of a job.

How you sell your property will be a personal choice. We do not have the time or patience to field all the calls and take the necessary steps to sell our properties FSBO, but placing a FSBO sign outside your property can save you thousands of dollars in realtor commissions. Be prepared for realtors calling you, attempting to get you to sign listing agreements with them. Some realtors will call, claiming to have a buyer for your home, and they will be more than happy to show their client your home if you sign a listing agreement. Some of these realtor calls are valid; others are misleading and nothing more than a baiting tactic.

If you are new to Tax Deeds investing, it is unlikely the money you are using is interest-free. Whether it is from an equity line, a loan from relatives, or a hard money loan, interest is accruing daily. Most of the time, there are "points" assessed with the loan. 1 point would mean that for every $100,000 you borrow, 1% is owed as a fee, or $1,000 in addition to the annual interest rate of, say, 12%. If you hold that loan for 1 year, you would pay $12,000 in interest plus 1 point equaling $1000, for a total of $13,000 in interest! It adds up quickly. Most real estate investors use the "burn and turn", or "flipping" approach. We attempt to put our properties for sale on the open market as quickly as possible, in order to reduce the amount of accumulating interest. Sometimes we go to the extent of finding buyers before we acquire the property.

The following information includes REAL figures from one of our properties.

4344 Middlebrook, Orlando, Florida

Purchase Price	$70,000.00
Title Clearing	$1,485.00
Points on Loan	$788.00

Interest	$1,044.00
Repairs	$2,614.00
Utilities	$245.00
Insurance	$451.00
Taxes	$2,091.00
Closing Costs	$6,892.00
Total Costs	$85,610.00
Sales Price	**$111,000.00**
Profit	**$25,390.00**

The reason we are including these details is because too many times we read examples that look more like this:

Bought:	$70,000
Repairs:	$2,614
Sold:	$111,000
Profit:	**$38,386.00**

We want to show you exactly what costs you will incur when buying and selling real estate. When evaluating your next property, make sure you consider these costs and to be safe, add in a little extra money for items you may overlook. Trust us, it will happen.

Evaluate each project's risk versus the acceptable amount of profit you hope to receive.

No two companies or people operate the same. Everyone calculates their required profit returns and acceptable risks in different ways. We have a friend that will do just about ANY deal if he can make $50,000. You might say, "Well, yeah! I'd like to make $50,000 too!" But what if you had to risk $800,000 to profit $50,000? Is that still a good deal? We have a different approach.

Our approach is to ask the following questions:
1. What is our potential maximum liability?
2. What will be our minimum profit?
3. What will be our maximum profit?
4. How long will the project take to complete and sell?
5. What will this profit allow us to do in the future?
6. Will we learn anything from this deal?
7. Will this open more doors or new contacts by doing this deal?
8. How will others perceive our company by completing this transaction?
9. Does this project benefit anyone besides our company?
10. Does this deal involve aspects that we do not understand?

11. What aspects of this deal that may affect us can we NOT control?

12. What is our cash on cash return on this deal compared to the risk involved?

13. What is the ANNUALIZED return?

14. Can we afford to take on this project?

15. If we cannot sell this project, what will we do with it in terms of renting, lease optioning, etc.?

These are some great questions you should think about before you complete a real estate transaction. Your risk-to-reward values may change over time. Ours certainly has.

What if, in the above example, we said you would have to put up $500,000 to make that $50,000? Some of you are already saying, "no way! What a bad deal!" Well, we would say you aren't asking enough questions. Maybe you only need to put up the $500,000 for two or three weeks to make the $50,000. Maybe your $500,000 is secured by a piece of property worth $1.5 million. Now is it a good deal? Again, you will have to answer that question yourself.

On a smaller scale, let's put up $5000 to make $500 in a two week period. That 10% return in two weeks is a non-compounded 260% return annualized!

CHAPTER 4

In this chapter, you will learn:

- Be wary of Code Violations
- Lien holder notifications
- How to deal with IRS and Home Owners Association Liens
- What happens to the original mortgage after a sale
- What are overages

Beware

There are many items to be aware of concerning Tax Deeds. The most dominant ones of are Code Violations, IRS Liens, Government Taxes, and CDDs.

Code Violations

The most common item to be aware of is code violations. Most of the time, these amounts owed by the property owner will show up on the title search, which the county should provide for you. For this reason, it is important to look through the title search to see what issuing authorities have issued liens and are demanding payments. There are many questions to be answered here:

1. What is the code violation for?
2. Who is the issuing authority?
3. What is the dollar amount?
4. Are the penalties accruing daily?
5. Is there interest accruing?
6. Can the violations be fixed?
7. If the violations can be fixed, how much will it cost and who will fix them?

The reason this is so crucial is because different authorities may or may not waive or reduce those fines. Some departments work strictly by the book, while others will remove the violation for $100, and some will remove the violation for a percentage of the penalty. Code violations stay with the property if they are not paid off from the sale proceeds, so be aware that these violations may exist.

If you do not perform proper due diligence, you may win a property at auction and then receive a County code violation bill for $10,000. Imagine how unhappy you would be to receive such a surprise.

Case Study

In January 2004, we attended our first Tax Deed auction in Polk County, Florida. Before the auction began, a woman from Polk County Code Enforcement Division announced that she would remove any code violation from any property for the amount of $100. She explained that even if the violations amounted to $10,000, $100 would be all that was needed to remove the lien. As it so happened, one of the properties we were bidding on was a building that had burned down. The only real value was in the land. There were many safety code violations attached to the property due to the owner not tearing down the structure. The fines totaled over $10,000. As it turned out, we were not successful in acquiring the property, but we had learned a valuable piece of information. We now had more buying power on properties that had code violations in that county, as we knew these county liens could be negotiated and removed easily. Other investors tend to be put off by government liens, so this reduced our competition.

Overages

Overages refer to the money that is received above the owed amount. The best way to explain this concept is through an example.

Example

Minimum Bid Amount:	$ 12,600
Final Bid Amount:	$100,000
County Fees:	$ 600
Total Amount:	$100,600
Total Overage Amount:	**$ 87,400**

We calculated the overage amount by taking the final bid amount ($100,000) and deducting the minimum bid amount and the county fees ($12,600 + $600 =$13,200). This means that there is an additional

$87,400 in overages that can be claimed by any party which considers itself to have legal rights to the money. This includes banks, mortgage note holders, other lien holders, and, of course, the owner of the property.

Let us now take this example one step further:

Total Overage Amount:	$ 87,400
Outstanding Mortgage:	$ 48,000
County Liens:	$ 1,200
HOA Liens:	$ 2,500

New Overage Amount: $ 35,700

In the second part of the example, we are assuming that the bank claimed the outstanding mortgage balance, and that all other liens were paid off. This would leave a total overage amount of $35,700. This money can then be claimed by the original owner of the property. The owner must make his claim within the county's allotted claim time. If the owner's claim is successful, the county will then mail him the final overage amount. If the owner does not make a claim, the money would be held by the local county for a set time period, after which the money would be kept by the county. The new owner of the property cannot make claim to this overage amount unless he has legal entitlement. There have been many instances where we have seen a huge overage amount remain unclaimed. So who was the lucky recipient of all this money? The local county!

Notifications to Lien Holders

When a property is scheduled to be sold at a Tax Deed sale, the county must provide all lien holders with adequate notification of the sale. These lien holders may include banks, mortgage companies, homeowners associations, governmental agencies, etc. This notification gives these lien holders an opportunity to pay off the owed taxes in order to prevent the sale of the property. In most cases, banks don't pay off the owed taxes because of the lack of equity in the property. Banks are not in the real estate business, so they would rather have the property auctioned and receive the overage money to pay off the mortgage note (read the overages section for more information). In rare cases where the mortgage balance is low and a lot of equity remains in a property, a bank may pay off the taxes to stop the sale.

This lien holder notification is a very important part of the Tax Deed process. There have been rare cases of court judgments overturning Tax Deed sales because of improper lien holder notifications. A failure to properly notify all lien holders is one of the few reasons why a Tax Deed property could be legally contested. Since the county keeps records of all its notification attempts, improper notification is a very difficult mistake to prove.

What happens to the Mortgage and other Liens after the property is sold?

This is an excellent question, and one that is asked quite frequently. All liens that are non-governmental are generally wiped clean. You read that sentence correctly! If the lien holders on a property choose not to act after notification, their liens will be lost after the property is sold. Realistically, in today's market, the overages will take care of most liens. Make sure you verify all information with your specific county.

Please remember that this is not the case for governmental liens. These remain attached to the property at all times. Some examples of government liens would be taxes, IRS judgments, and code enforcement violations. Sometimes it is possible to negotiate with government agencies to reduce these lien amounts or to have them attached to the owner rather than to the property. You should be prepared to pay any government liens in case negotiation isn't possible.

Let's discuss these possible liens.

Government Taxes & IRS Liens

Unpaid income taxes are common on larger or more expensive properties. We have seen past due income taxes amounting to hundreds of thousands of dollars. This means that in order to achieve clear title on the property, the IRS would have to be paid the amount they are owed. Sometimes this is achieved through the sale of the property, sometimes it isn't. Sometimes the old property owner has a high net worth, and the IRS can be convinced to attach the lien directly to the person and his or her credit rather than to the property. This is not usually the case, though; the government enforces the lien by attaching the owner's main asset, the home. This makes researching the title imperative. Imagine buying a home at a Tax Deed auction thinking you picked it up at a great price, only to find there is a huge IRS lien attached to the property!

Example

After researching a property, you find that the current owner owes $150,000 in back taxes. There is no current mortgage. The property you want to purchase at the auction is worth about $175,000. The minimum bid is $10,000 to pay off the tax lien with the fees. After computing profit, repair costs, holding costs, and selling costs, you calculate your maximum bid amount to be $145,000. If you bid up to the $145,000, the county will receive their $10,000 for the tax lien. The remaining $135,000 will go to the IRS for the back due income taxes, and then the IRS will impose the remaining $15,000 lien onto the property. There is a slim chance you could persuade the IRS to waive this and attach the lien to the previous owner. We find this deal to be very risky, as it means you would need to accept a lower profit or cut costs to make your numbers work. If you paid $145,000 for the property and incurred another $15,000 from the IRS, your new cost would be $160,000. This does not include your repair costs, holding costs, or selling costs. Your profit would be diminished or eliminated.

There are plenty of situations where the IRS tax owed will not be significant, but will still need to be taken into consideration. Our goal is to make you aware of this danger so that you can figure it into your bid calculations. These oversights or miscalculations can have a large impact on your bottom line profit, making the difference between a GREAT deal, an OK deal, and possibly not a deal at all.

Home Owner's Association (HOA)

HOA dues are another lien item that remains attached to a property after it is sold at a Tax Deed sale. These liens are held against the property, not the property owner, and usually these liens cannot be negotiated. After the Tax Deed sale, "overage" or additional proceeds pay off the remaining taxes, liens, and fees. These are paid in the order of filing dates with the county. If the overage does not cover the HOA fees, you as the new owner may have to pay them. Each state has different rules regarding past due HOA fees, so please check this information carefully and make sure you understand what you may be held liable for.

Case Study

In 2005, we purchased 1697 Waterview Loop in Polk County, Haines City, Florida for $210,400. We estimated its market value as somewhere between $315,000 and $330,000. After the auction, someone congratulated us by saying, "way to make $100,000 in a day, huh?" We could tell this was an inexperienced investor. An experienced investor would know there were many other expenses associated with this property, including overdue HOA fees, repairs, and realtor fees. As it turned out, the last person had paid $160,000 for this home 4 years prior. It was located in a very desirable gated golf course community. The overdue HOA fees totaled $3500, and, since we didn't want to pay the $3500, we assisted the HOA in claiming the owed money through the county's overage amount. Thankfully, the county paid the owed amount, so we did not need to worry about paying the $3500. If there had not been enough funds available to pay the HOA fees, the HOA would have imposed those fees onto the new owner of the property, and most likely charged additional fees and penalties to boot.

CDD

CDD stands for Community Development District. This represents a bond issued by a government agency which allocates funds for bringing in utilities to an area that is under development. An assessment is issued against each property to pay for the services brought to the development area. Interest payments are due on the CDD bond. As the developer sells off the lots, they can reduce the principle amount owed on the CDD bond. This reduction can also come in the form of assessments due annually, quarterly, or any regular time period. The property owner would have to pay those assessments each time they are due. This money usually goes towards the interest payments of the CDD. If the payments fall behind, the bond issuers can "call the bond due", which means that now ALL the money is due immediately. This can be devastating for the owner of the property, as they may not have the large amount of money needed to re-pay the CDD.

The following case study has been simplified so you can understand the concept. It is based on a real life situation in Lake County, Florida.

Case Study

Our company was interested in 14 lots coming up for auction in Lake County, Florida. The community was located on an island-type setting which included a gated golf course community surrounded by water with a two lane access road. Oddly enough, there were only 10 built homes out of the 400 or so lots. These homes were very high end, in the $400,000 to $1.5 million range. There were only 10 or so built homes in the neighborhood making the whole situation appear strange. We were willing to pay up to $50,000 per lot, but we felt more research was needed on the situation. After speaking with the Tax Deed office officials, we found out there were other properties that had already gone to auction in this neighborhood. There were very few bids on these lots, and some even had no bids.

Why wouldn't anyone want to bid on these seemingly desirable lots? We dug deeper and deeper into the title search, which contained over 300 pages of information (far more than normal, as most title searches contain 2 to 5 pages). We looked at EVERY page, and encountered something we had never seen before. There was a list of lot numbers with huge dollar amounts notations next to them. These numbers were $60,000 and higher. The total was over $3 million! We called some of the companies and people referenced in the title work, and finally contacted a person who knew what these numbers represented. As it turned out, a developer had received an approval for a CDD bond to develop the property. He completed all the utility work, including roads, lighting, water, and sewer. Then the developer went bankrupt and lawsuits were filed. The whole situation was a mess. After many phone calls, despite not knowing the right questions to ask, we finally stumbled upon a real estate broker who had worked out a deal with the insurance company holding the CDD bond. He had negotiated a discount with the bond holder on the liens attached to the lots, but it was still far from a good deal, in our opinion. For this reason, we declined to bid on the 14 lots, which turned out to be a wise decision. If we had been the winning bidder on these lots, we would have been liable for the attached CDD bond amounts also. These amounts ranged between $60,000 and $90,000 per lot. Ouch! Some of our competitors who purchased these lots were not as diligent with their research, and may have some on-going legal problems with these properties.

Again, make sure you look through all the title work the county provides. It is free information that can save you time, money, and headaches.

CDDs are not the only form of government liens that can occur. Be sure to use all the information that the Tax Deed office makes available to you. Through the years, we have seen many people make foolish buying mistakes. We never take pleasure in seeing others make mistakes, which is why we preach due diligence.

If something does not seem right, it probably isn't. Great deals do exist, however; we know this for a fact, as we come across them daily. Good deals can be found as long as you keep looking. This is true whether you are looking for them in the newspaper, researching Tax Deed auctions or researching foreclosure markets.

CHAPTER 5

In this chapter, you will learn:

- How to clear the title
- How to handle abandoned personal property

Obtaining Clear Title

I f you plan on selling the tax deed property you have purchased, this will be one of the most important sections you will read in this book.

Properties purchased at Tax Deed sales do not come with clear title!

What do we mean when we say a property has clouded title? When you purchase a Tax Deed property, the title that is issued is just that, a Tax Deed. It is not the traditional deed issued, such as a Warranty Deed or a Quit Claim Deed; it is not even a Special Warranty Deed. It is referred to in the real estate world as "Clouded Title".

Clouded Title is defined as an irregularity, a possible claim or encumbrance that, if valid, would adversely affect or impair the title.

Most title insurance companies will not insure a property that has a clouded title. It is important to know the basics regarding titles.

When you sell a property, most buyers will need to acquire a mortgage in order to purchase the property. When they finance that property, the bank requires title insurance. Title insurance "insures" that the chain of title from owner to owner is clear, and no one can come back to claim ownership of the property. The term "clear chain of title" means that all signatures are present, all current and previous owners are accounted for, and all debts and liens attached to the property while a previous owner held it were paid in full.

This is not usually the case with a Tax Deed property.

Why?

The owner did not sign a deed. The property was sold at public auction due to non-payment of real estate taxes. Most likely, there was a mortgage on the property which was not satisfied by the sale of the property. There may have been other debts that were not paid due to the sale of the property. These items create the clouded title.

What could you do with a property that has title issues or clouded title? Well, you could rent it, lease it, or live in it. You could also sell it to a cash buyer, but bear in mind that any person who cannot sell property to a buyer looking to finance the property will face difficulties. If you can only market your property to cash buyers, you are only marketing to a tiny percentage of the real estate world. This is a big mistake, and unless you are selling your property at a large discount, you may be sitting on it for a long time to come.

Case Study

John is a friend of ours who purchased a Tax Deed property in 2001. John had been renting his Tax Deed property on a month to month basis for a while, but then he attempted to sell the property on the open market through a realtor. When the realtor secured a contract, they went through the normal process of appraisal, inspections, etc. The buyer qualified for a mortgage with a broker and everything seemed to be proceeding well. When John picked his title company to complete the closing, they informed him that they would not provide title insurance on the property. Confused, he asked them why not, since he had kept insurance on the house for several years. John did not understand the difference between Homeowners Insurance and Title Insurance. Yes, John did have insurance on the property, but he did not have an insurable title. All traditional lenders will require title insurance. John was unable to sell the property until he obtained a clear title. This process took John four years from the date he purchased the property. Even though his property netted him a nice return in the form of rental income each month, John faced some severe challenges in reselling the property. As it turned out, he needed the money from the sale of this property in order to complete another transaction. John was uninformed about the other choices available in obtaining a clear and marketable title. Needless to say, he was not happy.

You don't have to be like John, because there are easy ways to obtain clear title on a Tax Deed property. Let's go through these choices and see which one will work best for you.

There are 4 routes to clearing a Tax Deed property title you can choose from.

1. Do nothing and keep the property as a long term investment, or sell to a "cash" buyer. This does not clear the title, but it avoids financing problems.

2. Wait a period of time, approximately 4 years, and then apply for a new title. This period of time varies from state to state.

3. Pay large attorney fees, and wait 6 – 12 months (or more) for Quiet Title services. This service is not even a guarantee you will receive clear title.

4. Visit www.taxdeedbook.com and find out more information about our recommendations for clearing the title in a cost-effective fashion, giving you the ability to resell your Tax Deed property in 60 – 90 days.

Let's look further into these four options:

Option 1: Do Nothing

This is pretty self-explanatory. You purchased the property at a Tax Deed sale and have all the ownership rights. You do not have to do anything to retain ownership. You could rent the property out, you could lease the property, or you could also live in the property.

If you are planning on selling the property, the type of title the county generally issues at the sale is not acceptable, due to the title insurance issues. You would need to choose one of the next three options. If you were fortunate enough to find a cash buyer and they were willing to accept the clouded title possibilities, then you may be able to proceed with the sale without clearing the title. However, this is a highly unlikely scenario, because most cash buyers will want clear title too.

Case Study

In June 2004, we purchased 8.8 acres of land at an auction in Seminole County, FL. The following day, we received a fax from a man offering to sell us 4 acres of land located behind our 8.8 acres. The man had purchased this property in 2002 at a Tax Deed auction and was having a difficult time selling it due to title issues and land accessibility. We paid $17,000 cash for his property, knowing that we could quickly obtain clear title. The seller was fortunate that this seemingly worthless piece of land was valuable to us, and he was also fortunate that we were a cash buyer who didn't need him to provide us with clear title on the property. If we had not been willing to buy the property, his $6000 investment would have been worth very little.

We personally do not like the "do nothing" option, because we want the option to sell our property quickly if need be. We are in the business of improving real estate, and the money used to purchase a property is precious. When there are plenty of deals available, we prefer to sell our properties and use our money several times per year, rather than using the money on only one or two deals a year. When good deals are harder to find, we may choose to use the "do nothing" option, but this is extremely rare. In most cases, we look at the other three options as these keep the properties in motion, allow us to refinance, and eventually to sell them. Now we can take that profit and invest those proceeds into a new property and begin the cycle again.

Option 2: Wait for 4 years

Depending on your state, after purchasing a Tax Deed property, you can wait a period of 4 years or so and then apply to the County for a clear title. We have never needed to go though this process, so please consult your real estate attorney if you choose this option for your Tax Deed property.

Even in the cases where we held a property for a long term investment, we still cleared the title with our 60 – 90 day system.

Why would we do that?

There is a very good reason to go ahead and get the title cleared. Clear title is not only useful when you sell the property, but is also required when you REFINANCE the property. Remember that you will be paying cash for the property and you will probably want some (or all) of your initial investment back.

How will you buy more properties if you plan on waiting 4 years to clear the title? Unless you have bank vaults full of cash (in which case we invite you to call us), you won't be able to purchase more properties, and your finances will be cut short for those 4 years.

Case Study

We have a business associate that purchases between 1 and 3 Tax Deed properties a year. Most of these properties are low income houses or are heavily dilapidated. He bids on properties that most people would shy away from, enabling him to purchase them for low prices. He purchases the properties to generate monthly income and for long term appreciation. Since he holds his properties longer, the taxes he pays on his gains are lower. He has quite a bit of extra cash and income from his regular job, and he chooses to invest all that extra money into his properties and rent them out. After 4 years, he applies for a new title in what is called a "Final Judgment" and then assesses whether or not he wants to sell them. This option is not feasible for most "burn and turn" or "flip" investors, as they do not have the resources to pay for properties with cash and then leave the equity in the property for 4 years.

Option 3: Hire an Attorney for Quiet Title

We have used this process only once. This is the most common practice for clearing a clouded title and is generally quite costly. Most attorneys will not be able to give a set price to achieve clear title because they don't know how much time will be spent on clearing the title, due to all the research and paperwork involved. Sometimes they are able to estimate a range of cost; however, we found this estimate to be much smaller than the actual end cost. Even though our attorney was able to deliver clear title, we can offer access to a system that will complete this task MUCH quicker and a lot cheaper.

Case Study

We purchased our first tax deed property in 2003 and had a great relationship with the original owner (read the Actual Stories chapter for more on this). After purchasing our property, we then became aware of the issues associated with clear title. As we were inexperienced at the time, we knew of few options for obtaining clear title, so we chose to hire an attorney to obtain Quiet Title. Since the original owner hoped to repurchase the property from us, he gave us all the time we needed and did not mind if the property took longer than normal to close. The buyer was financing the property, so the "do nothing" and "wait 4 years" options were not possible. Nowadays, we use our clear title system, which generally achieves the marketable title in a much shorter time period than Quiet Title.

Expect the Quiet Title process to take up to 12 months, or longer if problems like probate or divorce are involved. Quiet Title is successful in most cases, but you will need to arrange a consultation with a real estate attorney familiar with this type of procedure. We recommend you find a good real estate attorney anyway. At some point, you WILL need one.

Do not assume that your existing attorney will be able to handle obtaining a Quiet Title. If they say they can complete a Quiet Title, find out how many they have successfully completed in the past. What is their time frame? What will be the fees? What additional costs will you incur from the process? What will they do for you if they cannot clear the title? We have spoken to many attorneys who are not familiar with obtaining Quiet Title or do not handle these cases because of the amount of work involved.

Option 4: The 60 — 90 Day Process

This is the only technique we use for obtaining clear title for properties we purchase at Tax Deed sales. In most cases, we are able to obtain clear title in 60 to 90 days, sometimes in as little as 45 days. This technique is perfect for the real estate investor who wants to flip Tax Deed properties quickly. The process is simple and far more inexpensive than hiring an attorney. You mail in copies of your deed and all the county paperwork associated with the Tax Deed file and then the title can usually be cleared within 90 days.

Our website offers great rates for this easy to use service. Please visit **www.taxdeedbook.com** for more information. It is as simple as downloading a form and mailing in the paperwork.

Personal Property

We have encountered a few situations where Tax Deed properties we have purchased have contained personal property. In our Actual Stories section, you can read about two of these cases. At the time we wrote this book, the following applies in the State of Florida:

If you purchase a property at a Tax Deed sale, you are only entitled to ownership of the building and the fixtures. Fixtures are defined as anything permanently fixed or attached to the property. This would not include items such as refrigerators, furniture, and/or televisions. In Florida, the law requires you to advertise this personal property in the Public Notices section of the local newspaper for a set period of time, after which the personal property must be set outside the property. This is to give the owner an opportunity to retrieve these possessions.

Since we live in a "sue-happy society", always remember to list any personal property you recover in the local newspaper. In most States, this is law, and you don't want to be sued for disposing of someone's personal belongings. Please check the laws in the State where you are interested in purchasing Tax Deed properties, so you are familiar with the correct method of handling this issue. Understand that these recommendations are not intended to be legal advice. We have even gone to the extreme of video taping contents as soon as we gain access to the property. That way, if any arguments occur over personal property, we have proof of what was left in the home. Always perform your due diligence and understand your rights!

CHAPTER 6

In this chapter, you will learn:

- How to pay for Tax Deed properties
- Where to look for money to begin Tax Deed investing
- Why you should invest in real estate

Paying for Tax Deeds

In some counties, any property won at an auction must be paid for in cash. When we say cash, we mean some form of secured payment, such as a certified bank cashier's check or a money order. You can pay in the form of cash if you would like, but most counties would frown upon having to count out $100,000 in twenty dollar bills.

In Florida, if you are the lucky winning bidder, you must provide the auction officials with a $200 cash deposit. If you do not have the $200 cash deposit on hand, the county will re-auction the property immediately, so it is very important to attend each auction with enough cash. Each county's deposit requirements are different, so be sure to check before attending an auction.

Case Study

We have attended several auctions where the winning bidders have not been able to provide the auction officials with the required $200 cash deposit after winning the auction. One first-time bidder named Tony was so excited about acquiring his first Tax Deed property that he misplaced his wallet containing the $200 cash. Tony asked the auction employees if he could go to his car to search for his wallet, but the employees weren't open to this idea and informed him that if he could not pay the $200 cash deposit, the property would be re-auctioned immediately. Tony desperately asked other bidders in the room if they would be willing to loan him the $200 deposit, but, unfortunately, none of the investors were very receptive to helping

Tony out of his predicament because they wanted the property to be re-auctioned. What followed next was most amusing. One investor saw Tony's situation as an opportunity to make some money and offered Tony the $200 cash in return for a $1000 personal check. Although this offer seemed ridiculous, Tony understood the predicament he was in, and decided that this was the only way for him acquire the property. Before Tony could accept this offer, a bidding war occurred between the investors. Another investor offered Tony the $200 cash for an $850 check. Eventually Tony got his $200 cash in return for a $600 check. This was a win-win situation for all involved. Tony understood that even though he was paying $600 for $200, he would make far more than the extra $400 it cost him for his newly-acquired property. We believe he would have paid much more than $600 in order to get the $200 cash. Lessons to be learned here are always think creatively about possible solutions, and always attend a Tax Deed auction with plenty of cash!

Let us assume you have attended your first Tax Deed auction and you were fortunate enough to win a property. You have paid your $200 to the auction officials and obtained your deposit receipt. So where do you go from here? Let us also assume that you attended the auction in Orange County, Florida. Once you have paid your deposit, you have exactly 24 hours to pay the remaining amount of your bid. For instance, if the auction began at 10:00 am on a Tuesday (and ended at 11:30 am), then you have until 10:00 am Wednesday to pay the entire bid amount of your property. If you are not able to pay by the deadline date and time, you will lose your $200 deposit and you will not be permitted to bid at another Tax Deed auction in that county for one year. Once again, every county in every state has different regulations regarding non-payment, so be sure you are aware of this before you attend the auction. Make sure that when you bid on the property, you have access to the funds needed to pay for your entire bid amount. The county will tell you the total amount owed after you are the winning bidder. This final amount will include all the back owed taxes and county fees. Once you have paid the full balance owed, the property is yours! You will be able to proceed forward with your plans, but remember, if people are still residing in a Tax Deed property, you have to consult and follow your local laws before you can gain access.

How can I find the money to start Tax Deed investing?

This is the question we are asked the most. Money is easy to find if you know where to look. Sometimes it is right under your nose. You

do need cash to buy properties; however, even if your bank account is a little dry, here are some ideas on how to get started:
- Take out a home equity loan on your primary residence
- Partner up with a friend or family member who has money
- Partner with other Tax Deed Investors in other counties (finder's fees)
- Open a credit line at your local bank
- Use your savings
- Use your 401K or your retirement account
- Use Hard Money against your primary residence
- Credit Cards

Since we are here to bring you the truth about Tax Deed Investing, we won't blind you with promises of purchasing properties for "No Money Down". Some real estate books preach this method, and while it is possible, it is sometimes misleading and unrealistic, especially in today's real estate market. Some of these books were written in the 1980s when a real estate recession occurred. During that time, many people wanted to sell their real estate holdings, and because supply outweighed demand, there were many lucrative deals available. Depending on how the real estate market is doing at the time you read this book, deals may be plentiful or they may be scarce. Don't worry if the real estate market is flat! There are still deals to be found; you just have to dig a little deeper to find them.

Many people who have been seeing unimpressive returns on their stock market accounts have been turning to real estate because of its distinct advantages. Not only does real estate usually appreciate over time, it also has some relatively new tax advantages. Some areas of the USA have seen real estate prices increase more than 100% in one year, so you can see why people would turn to this investment.

Why banks don't work

During a visit to an auction, a new investor named Charlene asked us why she couldn't go to a bank to borrow money to pay for a Tax Deed property. The main problem is that banks will not lend money for these properties because Tax Deeds are not sold with clear marketable title. As we discussed earlier, since the property does not have marketable title, most insurance companies will not issue title insurance. This is crucial, because when you sell it, any financial company lending on a property will require title insurance.

The other issue we find is **seasoning issues**. Seasoning refers to the amount of time a property is held by the previous owner. Banks feel comfortable when a property is held for 6 months to a year before it is sold. They hate shorter-term real estate investment. This is one of the biggest hurdles to investing in this type of real estate.

When trying to acquire financing for a property, banks have certain rules and requirements that they insist consumers follow. Due to the short nature of payment requirements and unclear title, banks will not loan money on Tax Deeds. You can save time by looking below at our suggestions for alternative methods of financing.

Option 1: Take out a home equity loan on your primary residence (HELOC)

Your primary residence is the best untapped source for money. This can be your gateway to becoming a real estate investor. Most people do not know that they can use the equity they have in their home to invest in other businesses. Nearly every bank in the USA is advertising Home Equity Lines of Credit (or HELOC) at very low rates with zero closing costs. Some banks will loan up to 100% of your home equity, depending on your credit score; however, the norm is around 90%.

Case Study

John had his eye on a 2 acre piece of land that was due to be sold at a Tax Deed auction. This land backed up to his own home, so John was particularly interested in buying this property. The minimum bid on the property was $650, but John discovered that the market value was in the region of $40,000. John was a man of simple means who didn't have much extra money to invest in real estate. After doing his research, John decided he was willing to pay up to $30,000 for the land, but he needed a way to acquire the money. John's local bank offered him an Equity Line on his home. John had owned his own home for over 10 years and accumulated over $100,000 in equity, so the bank was willing to loan him 90% of this equity at an interest rate of 5%. This meant John had up to $90,000 to use to purchase his land. John ended up purchasing the property for $29,500 and used the remaining $60,500 to purchase 2 other pieces of land in his area.

HELOCs are our number one recommended way to access money to purchase tax deeds. They are very inexpensive, easy to acquire, and, at least at the time of publication of this book, carry reasonable interest rates. After you learn how to acquire clear title on your Tax Deed property, you can tap into the extra equity and even take out another credit line on the new property. There are multiple ways to keep taking out the new equity of the purchased property to expand your real estate holdings. This is more commonly known as **leveraging** in the real estate world.

Option 2: Partner up with another person who has money available

This is another great way to access funds to become a Tax Deed investor. Take a pen and paper and write down all the people you know who could be possible investment partners. Since the stock market has been performing so erratically, there are many people who are looking for safer investment opportunities. You could offer these people a guaranteed rate of return on their money or offer them a profit share. Depending on their involvement, we recommend offering a guaranteed rate of return. The reason we use the guaranteed rate is that we know upfront what the interest will cost us. If we borrowed the money and offered the investor a percentage of the profit, the investor may feel they have an input in the decisions about fixing and selling the property. We do not like hands-on partners, and we love the saying "too many cooks spoil the broth!" Silent investors are a real estate investor's best friend. The investors we use are happy to receive their guaranteed return from us, and every now and then, if we do well, we will give them a bonus. They do not expect this, but they sure do appreciate it. The investor does not need to know how much you are profiting on the deal. That is your business only.

A prominent lawyer friend of ours once gave us some great advice: **Never count other people's money**. This means, don't worry about what someone else is making on a deal; only worry about what you are making. This is especially true when it comes to investors. Make sure they worry about what they are making on their investment, not what you are making. Make sure you inform an interested investor that you have the means to pay the interest on the loan, and that it is secured by real estate.

Case Study

When we first researched Tax Deed investing, we realized the emphasis on paying for properties with cash and addressed the problem immediately. We formulated a list of 50 people who were potential investors and were fortunate enough to find an investor who was willing to lend us $150,000 of startup capital. The investor was number 46 on our list so if we had given up at number 40, we may never have gotten started.

Potential investors can be family members, friends who are professionals such as doctors, lawyers, or accountants, or even people from your local real estate investors club.

We want to say a few words regarding partnerships. Originally, our business consisted of 3 people. The 3rd person decided to cease his involvement in our business during our first investment. If you do get involved in a partnership with someone, make sure you have a written agreement which states exactly what your partnership entails, including all financial and involvement details.

When considering business partnerships, be sure to choose people who are like-minded. You do not want to be involved in a company where the partners are constantly at odds with each other. Business partnerships have many pitfalls, but as long as all parties involved leave the lines of communication open, partnerships can be very beneficial.

KEY POINT: Do not leave anything assumed; this is where the problems begin! We cannot emphasize this point enough!! Most of our mistakes in real estate investing happened because we made assumptions based on past experiences.

Option 3: Partner with other Tax Deed Investors in other counties

Another idea for partnerships is to offer other Tax Deed investors in other counties an "eyes and ears" service.

Case Study

One of the most successful Tax Deed investors we met was named Brian. Brian had a huge network of eyes and ears. Since Brian could only cover so many counties at once, many of his eyes and ears would complete research for him. This meant that Brian did not have to drive hundreds of miles to look at properties in counties that were far from his home. This enabled him to attend only the auctions where a viable deal existed. If Brian was successful in bidding on a certain property, he would then pay the person that brought him the deal a generous finder's fee. This type of partnership enables several beginners to become real estate investors without any considerable cash or risk.

In order to form such a partnership, you will need to attend different tax auctions, whether in your home county or a county on the other side of the state. Don't be afraid to talk to other auction attendees, as you will find most of them are open to partnership suggestions. Always remember these people are in the business to make money, so if you can provide them with another avenue to do so, they will be all ears!

Some of these investors may refuse to talk about "their" real estate transactions or the county they work in because they don't want to give out free information. These are probably the wrong people to deal with, as they are narrow-minded and do not see the big picture. They do not understand that by joining forces, there will be times where they may not have the capital needed to complete a transaction or vice versa.

Unfortunately, in the real estate business (and any business), you will found unscrupulous people who you would never work with. Always try to sit back and watch how these people treat their friends, business associates, and the staff running the auctions. Sometimes people can read like open books. Always be aware.

Sometimes partnering up doesn't really mean having a partner. We have friends that live in other counties and other states that we can call upon to drive by a property and take a picture to email us. This can be very helpful, saving precious time. We always give them a kick back if we purchase the property.

Option 4: Open a credit line at your local bank

If you already own and operate a business, this is a viable option to begin financing your real estate career. Most banks offer businesses Lines of Credit. If you have a good relationship with your banker, set up a meeting to discuss this option. Most Lines of Credit offer favorable interest rates and are quick and easy to obtain.

You will have to make the decision of how much information to disclose to your bank. If you go in the bank asking for a credit line to purchase real estate that does not have clear title, well, they may just say no. If you simply ask for a credit line and give them limited information about your plans, especially the detail that you are looking to buy some real estate, they may be more inclined to lend to you.

We believe in giving banks only the information they NEED. You should not volunteer more information than they absolutely need.

Use your savings

We know you have already thought about this idea, but we thought we should mention it, with one cautionary note. If you are going to use your savings to invest in a Tax Deed property, please make sure you retain an adequate reserve to carry your investment through troubled times. There are 2 important things we have learned about real estate:

1.   Projects always take longer than expected
2.   Projects always cost more than expected

With this in mind, we recommend you have a cash reserve large enough to carry your expenses for at least 12 months, so that you can feel comfortable should anything unexpected happen. These expenses should include interest costs, repair costs, taxes, additional holding costs, and utilities. Too many times, we have seen people use their savings to purchase property, only to leave them under-funded when their project is not completed on time. When an investor experiences a slow-moving real estate market or has to rely on slow contractors, the investor may wind up holding the property longer than originally planned. You must prepare for these situations.

Option 5: Use your 401K or other retirement account

Since the stock market has been performing inconsistently over the past decade, many people have been cashing out of their retirement accounts and have been using this money to invest in real estate. If you withdraw your 401K prior to reaching the age of 59 years and 6 months, you will be taxed on any gains you have acquired, so we do not recommend this. However, there are methods for you to use the money in your 401K as loan collateral. Some banks may be willing to offer you a Line of Credit in this manner. Learn which banks offer these programs. Search the internet and talk to your local bank representative to see if they offer such a program.

You can also talk to your CPA (Certified Public Accountant) regarding using a Self-Directed IRA. This would allow you to use your retirement account to purchase real estate. Most CPAs are not familiar with this technique. We suggest you use a CPA who specializes in real estate, as he or she should be familiar with Self-Directed IRAs and how they can benefit you. Most CPAs are only qualified to file taxes and give very general tax advice. Having a knowledgeable CPA is the key to running a successful real estate business.

Again, when finding a professional, ask them how many real estate investments they own themselves. Sometimes this question alone can tell you how qualified they are. We try not to hire people who do not put their own advice into practice.

Option 6: Use Hard Money against your primary residence

Let us start by explaining the term "hard money". Hard money lenders are private individuals or businesses that loan money to real estate investors. Hard money loans are relatively easy to acquire because they are not purely based on an individual's credit history, but based more on the property that the person is trying to acquire.

Hard money lenders tend to offer a 70% Loan to Value (LTV) ratio. This means that if the property is worth $100,000, the lender will loan you up to $70,000. This is beneficial to the lender because if the investor defaults on the loan, the lender now owns a property that is worth $100,000 that they essentially paid $70,000 for.

Many hard money lenders also charge percentage points origination fees. This can range from 1% to a more standard 5%. This means that if the lender loans you $100,000, you would be charged a $5,000 origination fee up front. Another point to consider is that hard money comes with a higher interest rate than conventional financing.

It is not unusual for an investor to pay up to a 25% interest rate for the privilege of borrowing hard money. At the time of publication of this book, 15% seems a standard interest rate. Many people see this high interest rate as a huge disadvantage to borrowing hard money. We do not agree with them, however. If you were looking for a loan over a long period time then higher interest rates make no sense. Hard money loans are designed as short term or bridging loans. They are used when you need to purchase a property quickly. We would recommend that after no more than 6 months you would either have sold the property or refinanced it, paying off the hard money loan in the process. Even if you kept the hard money loan for one year, the higher interest rate would not have an adverse effect on your profits.

Find out whether the hard money lender will loan you 70% of the VALUE or 70% of what you PAID for the property. Most lenders will lend against the lower of the two, usually the paid price. Seek out a lender that will lend against the value, as this will make a huge difference in the amount you can finance.

Let's look at a table showing the difference between a conventional credit line and a hard money loan. We will assume that you will be making interest-only monthly payments on these loans:

Loan Amount	Interest Rate	Origination Fee	Loan Length	Monthly Payment	Total Cost of Loan
$100,000	5% *	0%	6 months	$416.60	$2,500.00
$100,000	5% *	0%	12 months	$416.60	$5,000.00
$100,000	15% **	5%	6 months	$1250.00	$12,500.00
$100,000	15% **	5%	12 months	$1250.00	$20,000.00
$100,000	25% **	5%	6 months	$2083.33	$17,500.00
$100,000	25% **	5%	12 months	$2083.33	$30,000.00

*Denotes a Home Equity Line of Credit
** Denotes a Hard Money Loan

As you can see from the table above, the lower the interest you can obtain on the hard money loan, the better. The interest rate differences should not deter you from acquiring a hard money loan. The difference between borrowing $100,000 for 12 months versus 6 months at a standard 15% is only $7,500. Always keep in mind that if you did not have access to this money, you wouldn't be able to make any sort of a deal.

We call hard money loans a "cost of doing business". You have to use every tool available to you so long as it is within your budget. If you have the opportunity of buying a property for $100,000 which has a market value of $175,000, the extra $7,500 in loan costs won't adversely affect your profits. Again, we would recommend using a hard money loan as a short term solution. Most banks will be willing to write a loan once you have held a property for 6 months, fulfilling their seasoning requirements, so if your project is taking longer than expected to complete or you decide you want to hold on to a property for a long period of time, refinancing is the best option.

Credit Cards

Because of their high interest rates (up to 30%) we use credit cards as a fund raising last resort and only as a very short term solution. If we must resort to credit card usage, we make sure we have other finances set up within a 30 days period, so the credit cards can be fully paid off. Sometimes we may have a hard money loan in process that cannot be completed in time for an auction. In that instance, we may use credit cards to withdraw cash to pay for an auction property and then pay off the credit cards when the hard money loan is completed. If you are going to use your credit cards, use the internet to find ones with lower interest rates. If you have great credit, rates can sometimes be found as low as 9% on a long term basis and even lower on short term. If you have been a credit holder for a long period of time, be sure to call your card company and verify your interest rate because it may be higher than you think.

To recap, there are many opportunities to raise capital to purchase Tax Deeds for cash. Even though you may not have the money collecting dust inside your bank account, we urge you to think creatively (or "outside the box", as we like to say). Networking is an underused and powerful tool in the real estate industry; use it wisely and, before you know it, you will be making your very own Tax Deed purchases!

Why should I invest in real estate?

Since we are here to bring you the truth about Tax Deed Investing, we want you to understand that this isn't a "No Money Down" process. I'm sure there is someone ready to argue with us right now, saying that if they borrowed money from someone and purchased a property at the auction, then it would be "no money down" because they used someone else's money. Our point is that it does take money, no matter where you get it. And yes, there will be some owners who would be willing to sign over their home instead of letting the property go to auction. We do not focus on that type of acquisition.

We have read many books that preach the "No Money Down" scheme, and we have found most of them unrealistic, especially in today's real estate markets. Some of these books were written during the real estate recession of the 1980s. During that time, many people wanted to sell their real estate holdings; because supply outweighed demand, there were many lucrative deals to be had.

People who have been experiencing unimpressive returns on their stock market accounts have been turning to real estate because of its distinct advantages. Not only does real estate generally appreciate over time, it also has many tax advantages, some of which are relatively new.

With the introduction of Homestead Tax Laws, you can now sell your primary residence with no capital gains tax, providing that you have resided in the property for 2 years or more. This is an amazing investment opportunity. Imagine being able to live in a home for 2 years and then sell it for a tax-free profit (with limitations). You could move every 2 years and provide yourself with some fantastic extra income. Some areas of the USA have seen real estate appreciate more than 100% in one year, so you can see why people would turn to this type of investment.

Another great reason to choose real estate is financing. Here is a task for you to try. Dress up in a suit and tie and visit your local bank. Ask to speak to the loan officer in charge. Proceed to ask the loan officer if the bank will lend you $100,000 to invest in the stock market.

We predict that you will receive responses like these from the loan officer:

..."Of course, sir; please deposit $100,000 cash into a non-accessible investment account with our bank and we would be glad to loan you $100,000."

"When the Cleveland Browns win the Super bowl, sir" (sorry, Cleveland fans).

"When hell freezes over, sir."

The loan office will probably just say, "No".

Okay, we know our jokes are in poor taste, but we are trying to make a point here. Most banks won't loan you money to gamble on the stock market. Yes we do know you can buy stock "on margin", but banks will more likely consider loaning you money for purchasing real estate.

Imagine you wish to buy a property worth $100,000 in value. Most investment loans will require some sort of down payment which will range from 5% (if you are friends with the bank president) to a more common figure of 10−20%. Imagine only having to provide $10,000 to buy an investment worth $100,000 or more. In real estate you will hear people discussing their investment profits based on **cash on cash**. This means you are calculating your profits based on how much money you have invested into a project, rather than how the much the project is valued at.

Let's look at a common single family home deal to show you an example of a "cash on cash" calculation:

Property Purchase Price:	$100,000
Loan Amount	$ 80,000
Down payment:	$ 20,000
Expenses and repair costs:	$ 10,000
Sales Price:	$150,000
Loan Repayment	-$ 80,000
Down payment	-$ 20,000
Repairs	-$ 10,000
TOTAL PROFIT:	$ 40,000
CASH INVESTED:	$ 30,000

CASH ON CASH RETURN: 40/30 = 1.33 (133%)

Let us do the same calculation for an investment in the stock market:

Stock Equities purchase price: $100,000
Rate of return per annum: +$ 15,000
(Based on a very optimistic 15% return)

TOTAL PROFIT: $ 15,000
CASH INVESTED: $100,000

CASH ON CASH RETURN: 15/100 = 0.15 (15%)

Don't forget you will have to pay 20% capital gains tax on your 15% profit in your stocks (unless it is in an IRA account, then it is tax-free, providing your contributions are within the allowed yearly amounts). We don't know about you, but to us, the stock market investment doesn't look very attractive. There is money to be made in the stock market, but you have to be extremely well-educated in research techniques in order to pick out good stocks buy. In our opinion, researching a company's accounts is about as much fun as visiting the dentist.

With real estate, on the other hand, you still have to pay capital gains tax on your profit, but there are creative tax advantages you and your accountant can use to lower your taxable amounts. Such techniques include 1031 Exchanges and using your expenses to write off against your profits. One huge tax advantage in real estate investing is your mortgage interest. You can write off all your mortgage interest and expenses against your profits. Check with your CPA for exact details.

Let's take the above real estate example one step further and say you could complete 2 projects a year. Based on the same numbers, this would mean your cash on cash return would be 266%! The stock market is looking less and less attractive at its 15% return on investment annually.

We truly believe that investing money into equities is very much a gamble. We do not like the idea of having an uncontrollable investment. Several massive conglomerates have gone up in flames due to false or inflated accounting practices. It seems unthinkable, but at one time, these companies were staples of their communities, and now they no longer exist. People ask us all the time, "If you can't trust a billion dollar corporation to invest your money into, who can you trust?" That's the way we feel. You cannot trust anyone other than yourself to make solid investment decisions. Keep in mind that some people have undergone fast-paced training to become Financial Advisors within 3 months! How would you like to give $100,000 to a so called "Financial Advisor" only to have him tell you "I'm sorry, sir, but I didn't see the stock market crash coming"? It happened in the year 2000 and it will happen again.

Education is the key to any type of financial investment. Educate yourself on the investment you are looking to make. Do not rely on anyone else.

One of our favorite sayings is "TRUST BUT VERIFY".

You should do this with any investment you are planning to make. We urge you to verify everything that we tell you also. Taking someone's word for it can be an expensive mistake to make, especially in real estate.

Let's look at the advantages and disadvantages of investing in the stock market versus investing in real estate:

STOCK MARKET:

Advantages
- Opportunity to make large returns on investment
- Tax-free gains when trading inside an IRA account
- Low trading commissions
- You can buy stocks with ease from your own home, with no experience

Disadvantages
- You have no control over your investment's performance
- On any given day, your investment can lose all its value
- Lawsuits and bankruptcies negatively affect stock prices
- Difficult to finance money to invest in the stock market
- Standard returns are relatively low
- Worldwide events can negatively affect your stock's value
- Dubious accounting practices can affect your stock's valuation
- Unforeseen competitors can affect market values

- Inexperienced Financial Advisors can cause severe losses
- Lack of research can lead to poor investment choices
- You cannot insure against losses

REAL ESTATE:

Advantages
- Opportunity to make large returns on investment
- You have control over your investment
- Good real estate will always have value
- You can purchase insurance
- Can provide you with passive income
- Tenants pay your mortgage
- You can use your IRA account to purchase real estate tax-free
- Attractive cash on cash returns
- You can use OPM (Other People's Money) to purchase real estate
- Can appreciate over time
- Creative techniques can make property more valuable
- Tax advantages
- You don't need much capital to get started

Disadvantages
- Markets can turn against you
- Lack of research can lead to poor investment choices
- Can be expensive
- Dealing with tenants can be difficult

One thing you can always be sure of is that people need a place to live. Stocks are not a necessity, so when other investors decide to sell all their stocks in one day, it can have a detrimental effect on your portfolio. After the crash of 2000, many people who were close to retirement experienced the first disadvantage of the stock market:

You have no control over your investment's performance

This is the main reason we advise people not to invest in the stock market unless they have the money to lose.

CHAPTER 7

In this chapter, you will learn:

- Actual stories of our Tax Deed investing adventures
- Q and A session with a Tax Deed Official

Actual Stories

Here, we would like to share actual stories from some of our favorite properties purchased at actual Tax Deed sales.

Our Very First Tax Deed Auction!

When we began researching Tax Deed investments, there were no books or educational information about how the system works. Much of our information came from our own research and from annoying the local county tax officials to the point where they would answer our questions just to get us out of their offices. On September 23rd, 2003, armed with $100,000 acquired from an investor disheartened by poor stock market returns, we nervously entered the Orange County Tax Office for our first Tax Deed auction...

We had become relatively friendly with Tammy, who worked in the Tax Deed office and always greeted us with her usual friendly smile. She led us up the stairs to an office with about 15 chairs and enough standing room for 50 people. We watched as more and more people filled up the small office space. Eventually, about 80 people were crammed into the office, making us wonder if we had any chance of purchasing a property with all the competition.

Our list included 3 properties of interest, all of which we had viewed and assessed from the exterior for valuation purposes. The auction began at approximately 10:00 am. The first two properties were houses located in less-than-desirable neighborhoods in south Orlando, FL. We declined to bid on these because of our inexperience; we decided it would be better to bid on properties in better locations.

Those first 2 houses sold for relatively low amounts. The third property on our auction list was located on Basie Place in Orlando, FL. The property was a 1974 square foot, 4 bedroom, 2 bath house located in a blue-collar neighborhood in Orlando. We had driven by the house the day before, and it appeared to be in relatively good shape. The yard was neat and the exterior of the property was clean. The minimum starting bid amount was approximately $45,000. Tammy proceeded to announce the legal description and the bid amount. The room became silent.

We announced "Minimum Bid".

Tammy repeated our bid amount of $45,000 and just as we were expecting a barrage of bidders, Tammy said,

"Going once...going twice...sold to...?"

This was our cue to tell Tammy the name in which we wanted the house title to be recorded under. However, we were so stunned about winning the property that we stood there in silence.

Tammy once again said, "Sold to?"

and we finally blurted out "London Meridian".

We looked at each other in total disbelief. Laurence looked white as a sheet, while Matt's heart pumped full of adrenaline.
What just happened?
Did we just buy our first piece of real estate?
Why didn't anyone bid against us?
Did we just make a $45,000 mistake?
Did we do something wrong?
WHAT DID WE DO?

We nervously wandered over to the desk and handed Tammy our $200 cash deposit. She handed us a receipt and continued with the auction. We weren't sure how to proceed, so we made our way through all the onlookers and sat in the Tax Deed office contemplating the consequences of our purchase.

Why had no one else bid on this property? They must have known something we didn't. By now we were becoming very nervous and were eager to review the property's legal file to make sure we didn't overlook something. Eventually Tammy completed the auction and returned to where we were waiting. She informed us of the total owed amount and explained that we had 24 hours to make the full payment. Then she dropped the bomb on us.

"Why did you guys buy that house?"

Laurence looked pale, as if he was about to pass out.

"What do you mean? Why do you say that?" we asked.

"Well, no one else bid on it, so there must be a problem with the property. Usually, if it is worth anything, SOMEONE bids on it," Tammy replied.

Before going to the bank, we contemplated not paying for the property, losing our $200, and being banned from bidding at the auction for 1 year. We didn't know what to do! Matt believed that, since we were the winning bidders, the right decision was to proceed forward and pay for the property. Even if it had some major problems, there was enough room in the purchase price to make a profit.

We immediately went to the bank, got a cashier's check, and went back to see Tammy. Several other investors at the Tax Deed office asked us why we purchased the Basie Place property. By now we were very worried. We had only viewed the exterior of the house and had no idea what we would find on the inside. Was purchasing this property the right thing to do? We finally decided once and for all to pay for the property. We resolutely handed Tammy the full payment amount. From that moment on, we became 100% prepared to handle the challenges ahead. Tammy smiled as she accepted the check. From that point forward, we knew there was no turning back.

Tammy handed us our receipt, informed us that we would receive the deed within a couple weeks, and wished us good luck.

As we were walking to our car, a gentleman approached us; he was neatly dressed and very polite.

"Are you the guys that purchased the property on Basie Place?" he asked.

We answered yes, expecting some bad news.

"My name is Carl," he said, "It was my house you bought."

At that point, we were feeling mixed emotions. Our hearts sank, only to realize that the owner was present at the auction the whole time, waiting for his property to be sold.

Carl proceeded to explain his situation.

He had lived in the house for 45 years. It was his parents' house, and they left it to him when they died several years ago. Carl took out a home equity line of credit (HELOC) that did not have an escrow for taxes. He became confused when he received his tax bills at the end of the year. Due to his financial situation, Carl ignored this tax bill, which ultimately resulted in his house going up for auction to pay for the owed taxes. We felt very sorry for Carl, as he apologized for not paying his taxes.

Carl invited us over to the house so we could discuss his situation. We graciously accepted knowing this would be a great opportunity to assess the interior of the property and figure out if we could help him.

Most tax deed investors immediately begin the eviction process once they receive the deed to a property. **We believe this is inappropriate action, as we try to help out the individuals living in the house as much as we can.**

Two hours later, we arrived at our property. Carl invited us inside, and gave us a tour of the home. The house itself was in fairly good condition. It had a few leaks in the bathrooms and needed some updating, but other than that, it seemed in fine shape. There were no apparent disasters. From what we could see, we had stumbled into quite a good investment.

Carl explained that it would devastate him to lose his home, as the sentimental value alone was priceless to him. Eventually we bid farewell to Carl and agreed to let him reside in the property until a solution was found. On one hand we did not want to evict Carl, but on the other, we didn't purchase this property as a charity. After all, we were in the real estate business to make money.

Eventually we came up with a plan for Carl to remain in the property as a tenant at a monthly rental rate of $1000. This was approximately the same as his home equity line payment plus taxes and insurance.

We also presented Carl with a proposal where he would re-apply for another mortgage and re-purchase the property back from us at a price of $75,000. Since Carl's existing mortgage of $90,000 no longer existed and his obligations were released, we ASSUMED he would be able to apply for another mortgage and purchase his property back from us. After further research, we discovered that this was not the case.

Florida Law states that if a mortgage is written off due to the sale of a Tax Deed and the original owner re-applies for a new mortgage for the auctioned property, the originating lender can reinstate the original mortgage as a first position lien. This meant that if the original lender decided to pursue Carl, he would be obligated to make payments for the original loan and for any new mortgages on his property. This would be an easy way for Carl to owe far more than his property was worth, a position we did not want to see him in.

We then pursued the idea of selling the home to Carl's sister. This way, Carl could make the mortgage payments to his sister and the property would remain in the family. Unfortunately, Carl's sister had a poor credit score and was unable to qualify for a mortgage. After months without a solution, we decided to place the property up for sale. We knew that in fixed-up condition, the property had a market value of $120,000. We wanted to sell the property quickly, and, fortunately, our realtor was looking for an investment rental property to buy and hold. We sold the property to him for $95,000. Our realtor allowed Carl to remain in the home as a tenant, so this worked out well for everyone involved. Our realtor purchased a positive cash flow property that was worth considerably more than he paid, Carl was able to remain in his childhood home, and we made a nice profit.

We learned a very valuable lesson from this experience. After our auction purchase, other investors questioned us about why we purchased this property. This uncertainty made us uneasy, and our minds were filled with self-doubt. When you know you have diligently completed your research, trust your gut instinct. Always execute your own research so you can make your own decisions. Many people offer advice about things they have no or little knowledge of. It is easy to be put off or scared by someone else's negativity. How many times have you asked a friend about a business idea and had them reply "that will never work"? Next time someone recommends you don't make a real estate purchase, ask that person how many investment properties they own or have purchased. If we hadn't been committed to the purchase of our first property, we probably wouldn't have completed the deal, lost our $200, and not been allowed to bid for a year, and so, ultimately, we probably never would have become millionaires! Listen to your instincts!

As of the writing of this book, the Basie property value was assessed at $180,000. Some people thought we had made a mistake selling this property, because the value has risen so much. However, we believe that selling the house was the correct decision because if we had not sold the house, then we would not have been able to use the profit to pursue other properties and expand our company.

TAX DEED

STATE OF FLORIDA
COUNTY OF ORANGE

INSTR 20030547235
OR BK 07114   PG 3300
MARTHA O. HAYNIE, COMPTROLLER
ORANGE COUNTY, FL
09/23/2003 12:10:17 PM
DEED DOC TAX 318.50
REC FEE 6.00
LAST PAGE

The following Tax Sale Certificate Numbered 7746 issued on May 25, 2001 in the office of the Tax Collector of this County and application made for the issuance of a tax deed, the applicant having paid or redeemed all other taxes or tax sale certificates on the land described as required by law to be paid or redeemed, and the costs and expenses of this sale having been published as required by law, and no person entitled to do so having appeared to redeem said land; such land was on the 23rd day of September, 2003, offered for sale as required by law for cash to the highest bidder and was sold to:

LONDON MERIDIAN INC

ORLANDO FL 32807

Being the highest bidder and having paid the sum of his bid as required by the Laws of Florida.

NOW, this 23rd day of September, 2003, the County of Orange, State of Florida in consideration of the sum of Forty-Five Thousand Four Hundred Thirteen and-------------------------43/100 Dollars ($45,413.43), being the amount paid pursuant to the Laws of Florida does hereby sell the following lands situated in the County and State and described as follows:

LAKE MANN ESTATES UNIT NO 2 Y/96 LOT 1 BLK C 5482/4573 (PR98-888 LET ADM) OR B&P 6015/0030, ON 07-13-98, INST QC
PARCEL ID # 33-22-29-4595-03010

MARTHA O. HAYNIE, COUNTY COMPTROLLER
ORANGE COUNTY, FLORIDA

BY: _____
Deputy County Comptroller
Orange County, Florida

SEAL

WITNESS:

STATE OF FLORIDA
COUNTY OF ORANGE

On this 23rd day of September, 2003, before me, personally appeared C. Willis, Deputy County Comptroller in and for the State and County aforesaid, who executed the foregoing instrument, and acknowledged the execution of this instrument to be her own free act and deed for the use and purposes therein mentioned, who is personally known to me and who did not take an oath.

Witness my hand and official seal on the date aforesaid.

_____
Notary Public

Tax Deed File Number # 7746-2001

M. D. Ware
Commission #DD195445
Expires: Mar 23, 2007
Bonded Thru
Atlantic Bonding Co., Inc.

EXHIBIT H-1

HUD-1
A. Settlement Statement
B. Type of Loan

U.S. Department of Housing
and Urban Development

P. 2

OMB No. 2502-0265

		6. File Number	7. Loan Number	8. Mortg. Ins. Case Num.
☐ 1. FHA ☐ 2. FmHA ☐ 3. Conv. Unins.		3140		
☐ 4. V.A. ☐ 5. Conv. Ins.				
		10.		

C. NOTE: This form is furnished to give you a statement of actual settlement costs. Amounts paid to and by the settlement agent are shown. Items marked "(p.o.c.)" were paid outside the closing; they are shown here for informational purposes and are not included in the totals.

D. NAME OF BORROWER: ▓▓▓▓ a single man
Address of Borrower: ▓▓▓▓, Orlando, Florida 32806

E. NAME OF SELLER: London Meridian, Inc., Mathew Meridian, President
Address of Seller: TIN:

F. NAME OF LENDER: ▓▓▓▓▓▓▓▓
Address of Lender: ▓▓▓▓▓▓▓▓▓▓

G. PROPERTY LOCATION: 3310 Basie Place, Orlando, Florida 32805

H. SETTLEMENT AGENT: The Alien Law Firm, P.A.
Place of Settlement: 2800 Winter Lake Road, Lakeland, Florida 33803   TIN:
                                                                           Phone: 863-665-7220

I. SETTLEMENT DATE: 5/19/04   DISBURSEMENT DATE: 5/19/04

J. Summary of borrower's transaction		K. Summary of seller's transaction	
100. Gross amount due from borrower:		400. Gross amount due to seller:	
101. Contract sales price	95,000.00	401. Contract sales price	95,000.00
102. Personal property		402. Personal property	
103. Settlement charges to borrower (Line 1400)	135.50	403.	
104.		404.	
105.		405.	
Adjustments for items paid by seller in advance		Adjustments for items paid by seller in advance	
106. City/town taxes		406. City/town taxes	
107. County taxes		407. County taxes	
108. Assessments		408. Assessments	
109.		409.	
110.		410.	
111.		411.	
112.		412.	
120. Gross amount due from borrower:	95,135.50	420. Gross amount due to seller:	95,000.00
200. Amounts paid by or in behalf of borrower:		500. Reductions in amount due to seller:	
201. Deposit or earnest money		501. Excess deposit (see instructions)	
202. Principal amount of new loan(s)		502. Settlement charges to seller (line 1400)	2,653.85
203. Existing loan(s) taken subject to		503. Existing loan(s) taken subject to	
204. Principal amount of second mortgage		504. Payoff of first mortgage loan	
205.		505. Payoff of second mortgage loan	
206.		506. Deposits held by seller	
207. Principal amt of mortgage held by seller		507. Principal amt of mortgage held by seller	
208.		508.	
209.		509.	
Adjustments for items unpaid by seller		Adjustments for items unpaid by seller	
210. City/town taxes		510. City/town taxes	
211. County taxes from 01/01/04 to 05/19/04	442.24	511. County taxes from 01/01/04 to 05/19/04	442.24
212. Assessments		512. Assessments	
213. Rent credit from from 05/19/04 to 05/23/04	129.04	513. Rent credit from from 05/19/04 to 05/23/04	129.04
214.		514.	
215.		515.	
216.		516.	
217.		517.	
218.		518.	
219.		519.	
220. Total paid by/for borrower:	571.28	520. Total reductions in amount due seller:	3,225.13
300. Cash at settlement from/to borrower:		600. Cash at settlement to/from seller:	
301. Gross amount due from borrower (line 120)	95,135.50	601. Gross amount due to seller (line 420)	95,000.00
302. Less amount paid by/for borrower (line 220)	(571.28)	602. Less total reductions in amount due seller (line 520)	(3,225.13)
303. Cash (☑ From ☐ To) Borrower:	94,564.22	603. Cash (☑ To ☐ From) Seller:	91,774.87

Substitute Form 1099 Seller Statement: The information contained in blocks E, G, H, and I and on line 401 is important tax information and is being furnished to the IRS. If you are required to file a return, a negligence penalty or other sanction will be imposed on you if this item is required to be reported and the IRS determines that it has not been reported.

Seller Instructions: If this real estate was your principal residence, file Form 2119, Sale or Exchange of Principal Residence, for any gain, with your tax return; for other transactions, complete the applicable parts of Form 4797, Form 6252 and/or Schedule D (Form 1040).

Borrower's Initial(s):   Seller's Initial(s):

5.00/7.00 EA   DoubleTime®

A Condo in the Sun

We were looking to bid on a lakefront vacation condo in Orlando that was scheduled to be sold in the upcoming week. The 2 bed, 2 bath condo appeared to be in very good condition, and we really liked the location due to its close proximity to Universal Studios and Disney World. The condo was on the ground floor, so we were able to peek in through the windows to get an idea of the interior condition. The condition appeared to be immaculate and it was even fully furnished! The condo complex had wonderful community amenities such as a swimming pool and a tennis court area.

We valued this condo between $100,000 and $110,000, which, on the surface, seemed like a great deal. The starting bid amount was approximately $37,000. For 2 days we watched the auction listings and crossed our fingers that the condo would not be removed from the auction list. Our research showed the owner lived out of state, so we thought there was a good possibility of the condo being sold.

As luck would have it, our reasoning was correct. The owner did not pay off the taxes and the property was auctioned. This auction did not go as smoothly as our Basie Place auction, and we became involved in a back and forth bidding war with several other parties. Eventually we were victorious in our bidding efforts, and we purchased the property for $70,000. We were ecstatic, but we were also somewhat concerned, because the property sold for much less than we had anticipated. We probably would have paid $10,000 more for this condo unit.

We paid the bid amount in full, and drove down to the condo to view the interior condition. When you purchase a property via a Tax Deed sale, you don't get access to the property in the form of a key, so you usually need a locksmith. Once we provided proof of ownership, our locksmith provided us with entry.

Upon entering for the first time, we were ecstatic to find everything in near-perfect condition. All the bedrooms were furnished, electricity and water utilities were still connected, and there was even beer in the fridge! We looked for something that would give us an indication of when the condo was last occupied. Looking through the paperwork in the drawers, we discovered that this condo had been owned by an out of state businessman who offered it to his clients for vacation use and rented it out on a weekly basis.

The next problem for us to solve was the furniture situation. Legally, we weren't sure who the furniture belonged to. After some research, we discovered we had no entitlement.

When you purchase a Tax Deed property, you are not entitled to any personal possessions that remain inside or outside the property, including furniture. During the title clearing process, the owner was contacted and notified of the sale and the furniture situation. We offered to purchase the furniture from the owner, but he did not want to sell.

The owner was upset about losing the property. He contacted his attorney, who brought him up to speed on what happened, and he accepted this outcome. In this case, the owner did not owe a mortgage, so he was able to collect the overage amount from the county and put those funds towards purchasing another condo in the same neighborhood. The furniture was eventually moved into his new condo. After some minor cosmetic updating, such as carpeting and paint, we sold the property 3 months later for $111,000.

Approximately 100 people attended this particular auction, but strangely enough, only a handful of people actually bid on the properties. This is the norm with Tax Deed sales. Most people are there for observation purposes only. After you attend a few, it will become obvious who the serious bidders are.

TAX DEED

INSTR   20030566831
OR BK 07128   PG 0086
MARTHA O. HAYNIE, COMPTROLLER
ORANGE COUNTY, FL
09/30/2003 12:07:57 PM
DEED DOC TAX 490.00
REC FEE 6.00
LAST PAGE

STATE OF FLORIDA
COUNTY OF ORANGE

The following Tax Sale Certificate Numbered **8883** issued on **May 25, 2001** in the office of the Tax Collector of this County and application made for the issuance of a tax deed, the applicant having paid or redeemed all other taxes or tax sale certificates on the land described as required by law to be paid or redeemed, and the costs and expenses of this sale, and due notice of sale having been published as required by law, and no person entitled to do so having appeared to redeem said land; such land was on the 30th day of **September, 2003**, offered for sale as required by law for cash to the highest bidder and was sold to:

LONDON MERIDIAN INC

ORLANDO, FL 32807

Being the highest bidder and having paid the sum of his bid as required by the Laws of Florida.

NOW, this 30th day of **September, 2003**, the County of Orange, State of Florida in consideration of the sum of **Seventy Thousand** and------------------------00/100 Dollars (**$70,000.00**), being the amount paid pursuant to the Laws of Florida does hereby sell the following lands situated in the County and State and described as follows:

THE FOUNTAINS UNIT 3 CONDO CB 9/22 BLDG 3 UNIT 4344 3581/963
PARCEL ID # 07-23-29-8008-34344

MARTHA O. HAYNIE, COUNTY COMPTROLLER
ORANGE COUNTY, FLORIDA

BY:_____
Deputy County Comptroller
Orange County, Florida

SEAL

WITNESS:

STATE OF FLORIDA
COUNTY OF ORANGE

On this 30th day of **September, 2003**, before me, personally appeared **C. Willis**, Deputy County Comptroller in and for the State and County aforesaid, who executed the foregoing instrument, and acknowledged the execution of this instrument to be her own free act and deed for the use and purposes therein mentioned, who is personally known to me and who did not take an oath.

Witness my hand and official seal on the date aforesaid.

_____
Notary Public

Tax Deed File Number # 8883-2001

M. D. Ware
Commission #DD195445
Expires: Mar 23, 2007
Bonded Thru
Atlantic Bonding Co., Inc.

EXHIBIT I-1

$124,845

FOR SALE

4344 Middlebrook Orlando, FL 32822

- 2 bedroom, 2 bath condominium
- 1085 sq. feet
- Brand new carpet
- Brand new ceramic tile in kitchen and bathroom
- New Italian tile in 2nd bathroom
- 2 Master suites
- Waterfront view
- Highly desirable location
- Access to tennis courts and pool areas
- Includes all appliances
- Quick move in

All the following conveniences are close by:
- 15 mins from Disney and downtown Orlando
- 2 miles to Universal Studios, 1 mile to I-4
- 1 mile to Millennia Mall, Publix, Blockbuster, Home Depot, Pappa Johns, Eckerds, Expo, Amsouth Bank

FOR MORE INFORMATION CONTACT MATT

EXHIBIT I-2   **TEL:** ████████████

OMB Approval No. 2502-0265		

A. Settlement Statement

B. Type of Loan

1-5. Loan Type Conv. Unins.

First American Title Insurance Company
Settlement Statement

6. File Number 2027-454124-0716

7. Loan Number 204-185009

8. Mortgage Insurance Case Number

C. **Note:** This form is furnished to give you a statement of actual settlement costs. Amounts paid to and by the settlement agent are shown. Items marked "(POC)" were paid outside the closing; they are shown here for informational purposes and are not included in the totals. Amounts shown as RSL were retained by lender and deducted from the loan proceeds prior to receipt by settlement agent.

D. **Name of Borrower:**
Orlando, FL 32701

E. **Name of Seller:** London Meridian, Inc.
Orlando, FL 32807

F. **Name of Lender:** AMNET Mortgage, Inc., D/B/A American Mortgage Network Of Florida
10421 Wateridge Circle, Suite 250
San Diego, CA 92121

G. **Property Location:** 4344 Middinbrook Road, Orlando, FL 32811

H. **Settlement Agent:** First American Title Insurance Company
Address: 206 West Oak Street, Suite B, Kissimmee, FL 34741

I. **Settlement Date:** 03/26/2004

Place of Settlement Address: 206 West Oak Street, Suite B, Kissimmee, FL 34741

Print Date: 03/25/2004, 2:44 PM

Disbursement Date: 03/26/2004

J. Summary of Borrower's Transaction		K. Summary of Seller's Transaction	
100. Gross Amount Due From Borrower		400. Gross Amount Due To Seller	
101. Contract Sales Price	111,000.00	401. Contract Sales Price	111,000.00
102. Personal Property		402. Personal Property	
103. Settlement charges to borrower (line 1400)	4,999.64	403. Total Deposits	
104.		404.	
105.		405.	
Adjustments for items paid by seller in advance		Adjustments for items paid by seller in advance	
106. City/town taxes		406. City/town taxes	
107. County taxes		407. County taxes	
108. Assessments		408. Assessments	
109. Association Dues 03/26/04 to 04/01/04 @$180.00/mo	31.56	409. Association Dues 03/26/04 to 04/01/04 @$180.00/mo	31.56
110.		410.	
111.		411.	
112.		412.	
113.		413.	
114.		414.	
115.		415.	
120. Gross Amount Due From Borrower	116,031.20	420. Gross Amount Due To Seller	111,031.56
200. Amounts Paid By Or In Behalf of Borrower		500. Reductions In Amount Due to Seller	
201. Deposit or earnest money	1,000.00	501. Excess deposit (see instructions)	
202. Principal amount of new loan(s)	88,800.00	502. Settlement charges (line 1400)	6,891.45
203. Existing loan(s) taken subject		503. Existing loan(s) taken subject	
204.		504. Payoff of first mortgage loan	
205.		505. Payoff of second mortgage loan	
206.		506. Tax Installment: Amount to Orange County Tax Collector	1,695.86
207.		507.	
208.		508.	
209.		509.	
Adjustments for items unpaid by seller		Adjustments for items unpaid by seller	
210. City/town taxes		510. City/town taxes	
211. County taxes 01/01/04 to 03/26/04 @$1695.86/yr	394.93	511. County taxes 01/01/04 to 03/26/04 @$1695.86/yr	394.93
212. Assessments		512. Assessments	
213.		513.	
214.		514.	
215.		515.	
216.		516.	
217.		517.	
218.		518.	
219.		519.	
220. Total Paid By/For Borrower	90,194.93	520. Total Reduction Amount Due Seller	8,982.24
300. Cash At Settlement From/To Borrower		600. Cash At Settlement To/From Seller	
301. Gross amount due from Borrower (line 120)	116,031.20	601. Gross amount due to Seller (line 420)	111,031.56
302. Less amounts paid by/for Borrower (line 220)	90,194.93	602. Less reductions in amounts due to Seller (line 520)	8,982.24
303. Cash (X From) (To) Borrower	25,836.27	603. Cash (X To) (From) Seller	102,049.32

The HUD-1 Settlement Statement which I have prepared is a true and accurate account of this transaction. I have caused or will cause the funds to be disbursed in accordance with this statement.

Settlement Agent: _____ Date: _____

* See Supplemental Page for details.

EXHIBIT I-3

What Shall We Do With All that Junk?

One of the more interesting properties we purchased was located in Deltona, FL. After successfully bidding $60,000 on a 2 bed, 1 bath house, we made the one hour drive to the property and knocked on the door. We were a little hesitant about purchasing this property because of the commuting difficulties we would face if we decided to repair the property ourselves. We favor purchasing real estate in close proximity to our homes so we can keep on eye on the property, especially if tenants are involved.

When we knocked at the door, there was no answer; so we peeked through the window. It was difficult to see anything because the living room was very dark. However, there was a light on and it appeared as if someone was living in the house. We decided to leave a note in the mailbox rather than gaining forced access to the property. The note explained the situation and asked whoever was living in the house to call us immediately.

After 3 days of no contact, we decided to make an evening trip to the home to see if we could speak to the resident. We eventually managed to get the resident, Greg, to open the door. We explained the situation to him and asked if we could come inside to view the property. Reluctantly, Greg let us inside.

Unlike other properties we had purchased in the past, this property was in very poor condition. There was garbage covering most of the floors, and broken appliances and car parts littering the kitchen. There were dead insects throughout the bathrooms. The stench of the property was nauseating. Even though the property was a disaster area, we knew it was salvageable.

We asked Greg if he had been the owner of the property, and he told us he was just a renter who paid $400 a month rent. He explained to us he was unemployed at the present time. By now the warning bells were ringing in our heads; it looked like Greg was going to be a problem. We asked him if he wanted to remain living in the property, to which he replied yes. We explained that the rent would need to be raised and we would want to clean up the property. Greg said he also worked construction and that he would be willing to work on repairing the property in return for a rent freeze.

We had Greg sign a 1 year lease, and left the property feeling somewhat apprehensive. Our reservations about Greg became apparent around rent payment time. Greg did not have a phone, so contacting him involved making the hour-long drive to Deltona. This proved to be difficult, as most of the time, Greg was either not home or did not want to answer the door.

One week after no payment and no contact from our new tenant, we filed our eviction papers at the local courthouse. Eviction is something we try to avoid, but we understand that there are people out there who will take advantage of others. Since Greg was one of these people, we had to take a stern approach. He was served notice to leave and eventually did so. This was our first eviction, and, to date, the only eviction we have had to perform. Unfortunately, Greg did not take most of his belongings with him, so we rented a 30 yard dumpster and filled it to the brim with all of his garbage. He left behind 10 tons of garbage in total!

A few of Greg's belongs that we deemed as valuable, we advertised in the local newspaper. This gave him the opportunity to pick up his belongs if he chose to do so. Greg never returned for any of his possessions, so eventually they were stored outside the house. We have never seen anyone accumulate so much garbage in such a small living area. 10 tons of garbage in an 800 square foot space! We disposed of an assortment of random worthless items, included car engines, lawn mowers, 12-year-old newspaper coupons, empty beer bottles, and 2-year-old perishable food, including milk. It was a sight we hope to never see again. The living area was so dirty, looking at it made us feel physically ill. We were sick for 3 days after the clean up.

As it turned out, Greg was the owner of the property; his ex-wife deeded the home to him upon their divorce. It seems he did not have the ability to pay his property taxes. Although we felt bad for Greg's situation, we offered him a good alternative, which he declined to act upon. Unfortunately, as much as we try to help, some people choose not to be helped.

We eventually cleaned out the property and sold it to another investor who wanted to repair it for use as a rental. We sold the property for $65,000 in as-is condition.

06/01/2004 11:28 AM
Doc stamps 322.00
(Transfer Amt $ 46000)
Instrument# 2004-135203
Book: 5332
Page: 2370

DR-506

Tax Deed File No. __5311-00__

Property Identification No. ___8130-01-12-0160___

TAX DEED

State of Florida
County of Volusia

The following Tax Sale Certificate Numbered __5311-00__ issued on __MAY 29TH, 2001__ was filed in the office of the tax collector of this County and application made for the issuance of a tax deed, the applicant having paid or redeemed all other taxes or tax sale certificates on the land described as required by law to be paid or redeemed, and the costs and expenses of this sale, and due notice of sale having been published as required by law, and no person entitled to do so having appeared to redeem said land; such land was on the __01ST__ day of __JUNE__, __2004__, offered for sale as required by law for cash to the highest bidder and was sold to __LONDON MERIDIAN INC__ whose address is _____ __ORLANDO FL 32807__ , being the highest bidder and having paid the sum of their bid as required by the Laws of Florida. NOW, on this __01ST__ day of __JUNE__, __2004__, in the County of Volusia, State of Florida, in consideration of the sum of ($__46,000.00__) FORTY SIX THOUSAND AND NO/100 __*__ __*__ Dollars, being the amount paid pursuant to the Laws of Florida does hereby sell the following lands situated in the County and State aforesaid and described as follows:

LOT 16 BLK 12 DELTONA LAKES UNIT 1 MB 25 PGS 96 TO 100 INC PER OR 3899 PG 4076

Diane M. Matousek,
Clerk of the Circuit Court of Volusia County

By: _____
D L RUEGGER, Deputy Clerk
Volusia County, Florida

Witness: _____
PAT MATZINGER
_____
LORI DIGGS

STATE OF FLORIDA
COUNTY OF VOLUSIA
On this __01ST__ day of __JUNE__, __2004__, before me __KAREN CHITTY__ personally appeared __D L RUEGGER__, __Deputy__ Clerk of the Circuit Court or County Comptroller in and for the State and this County known to me to be the person described in, and who executed the foregoing instrument, and acknowledged the execution of this instrument to be their own free act and deed for the use and purposes therein mentioned. Witness my hand and official seal date aforesaid.

KAREN J. CHITTY
MY COMMISSION # CC 990847
EXPIRES: April 29, 2005
Bonded Thru Notary Public Underwriters

CL-0009-8412

EXHIBIT J-1

569 E. Normandy Blvd
Deltona, FL 32725

- Address: 569 E normandy Blvd Deltona FL 32725
  Parcel ID: 30-18-31-01-12-0160 (Volusia County)

- Details: 2 Bed 1 bath SFH. 841 heated sq. ft. Easy
  cosmetic rehab. Paint and carpeting etc. Fast
  growing area, comps are $80k +. Very close to I-4.

- Price: $65,000 cash or $69,000 with owner financing, $4,000 down 15% int. 6 month balloon.

FOR SALE

For more information please contact:
Phone: ████████████
Web: www.londonmeridian.com
Email: info@londonmeridian.com

EXHIBIT J-2

A. Settlement Statement			OMB Approval No. 2502-0265	
			B. Type of Loan	
Associated Land Title Group, Inc. **Final Statement**			1-5. Loan Type Conv. Unins.	
			6. File Number 1016-692918	
			7. Loan Number 500441814	
			8. Mortgage Insurance Case Number	

C. Note: This form is furnished to give you a statement of actual settlement costs. Amounts paid to and by the settlement agent are shown. Items marked "POC" were paid outside this closing, they are shown here for informational purposes and are not included in the totals.

D. Name of Borrower:

E. Name of Seller: London Meridian Inc.
███████ FL 32807

F. Name of Lender: Flagstar Bank, FSB
5151 Corporate Drive
Troy, MI 48098-2639

G. Property Location: 569 E. Normandy Boulevard, Deltona, FL 32725

H. Settlement Agent: Associated Land Title Group, Inc.
Address: 813 Deltona Boulevard, Suite A, Deltona, FL 32725

Place of Settlement Address: 813 Deltona Boulevard, Suite A, Deltona, FL 32725

I. Settlement Date: 12/28/2004
Print Date: 12/20/2004, 10:33 AM
Disbursement Date: 12/29/2004

J. Summary of Borrower's Transaction		K. Summary of Seller's Transaction	
100. Gross Amount Due From Borrower		400. Gross Amount Due To Seller	
101. Contract Sales Price	65,000.00	401. Contract Sales Price	65,000.00
102. Personal Property		402. Personal Property	
103. Settlement charges to borrower (line 1400)	3,340.27	403. Total Deposits	
104.		404. Policy Credit from Tax Title Services	264.50
105.		405.	
Adjustments for items paid by seller in advance		Adjustments for items paid by seller in advance	
106. City/town taxes		406. City/town taxes	
107. County taxes 12/20/04 to 12/31/04 @$1269.53/yr	41.74	407. County taxes 12/20/04 to 12/31/04 @$1269.53/yr	41.74
108. Assessments		408. Assessments	
109.		409.	
110.		410.	
111.		411.	
112.		412.	
113.		413.	
114.		414.	
115.		415.	
120. Gross Amount Due From Borrower	68,382.01	420. Gross Amount Due To Seller	65,306.24
200. Amounts Paid By Or In Behalf of Borrower		500. Reductions In Amount Due to Seller	
201. Deposit or earnest money	500.00	501. Excess deposit (see instructions)	
202. Principal amount of new loan(s)	58,500.00	502. Settlement charges (line 1400)	4,013.75
203. Existing loan(s) taken subject		503. Existing loan(s) taken subject	
204. Closing Cost Credit from Seller to Buyer	1,300.00	504. Payoff of first mortgage loan	
205.		505. Payoff of second mortgage loan	
206.		506. Closing Cost Credit from Seller to Buyer	1,300.00
207.		507. Disbursed as Proceeds ($500.00)	
208.		508.	
209.		509.	
Adjustments for items unpaid by seller		Adjustments for items unpaid by seller	
210. City/town taxes		510. City/town taxes	
211. County taxes		511. County taxes	
212. Assessments		512. Assessments	
213.		513.	
214.		514.	
215.		515.	
216.		516.	
217.		517.	
218.		518.	
219.		519.	
220. Total Paid By/For Borrower	60,300.00	520. Total Reduction Amount Due Seller	5,313.75
300. Cash At Settlement From/To Borrower		600. Cash At Settlement To/From Seller	
301. Gross amount due from Borrower (line 120)	68,382.01	601. Gross amount due to Seller (line 420)	65,306.24
302. Less amounts paid by/for Borrower (line 220)	60,300.00	602. Less reductions in amounts due to Seller (line 520)	5,313.75
303. Cash (X From) (To) Borrower	8,082.01	603. Cash (X To) (From) Seller	59,992.49

The HUD-1 Settlement Statement which I have prepared is a true and accurate account of this transaction. I have caused or will cause the funds to be disbursed in accordance with this statement.
Settlement Agent: _____ Date: _____

* See Supplemental Page for details

EXHIBIT J-3

A Fortunate Mistake

Yes we admit it, even we make mistakes. Even though we have never made a costly mistake in our investments, seasoned real estate professionals such as ourselves trip up occasionally.

It was a very hot summer day, and we had a long list of upcoming properties in Volusia and Osceola Counties that we needed to view. Unfortunately, we had procrastinated, and left all the viewings to the day before the auctions. Because two auctions were scheduled on the same day at the same times, we needed to split up and attend one auction each.

Now let's be honest: no one likes to work on a Sunday. But such is the nature of owning your own business; sometimes you have to make small sacrifices. We dragged ourselves out of bed at 7:00 am and made the 60 minute drive to the Kissimmee / Disney World area. As the day progressed, we completed the viewings of the Osceola County properties, but found we were making slow headway with the 14 properties we needed to view in Volusia County. The problem was that Volusia County is quite spread out, and all the properties were dotted around in inconvenient locations. The drive from Osceola to Volusia alone was 75 minutes. By the time the sun had set, we had viewed only 10 properties. We wrote off the last 4, because our general rule is to never buy anything sight unseen.

When we returned to our office, we looked through all of our notes, and noticed that one of the properties we didn't have time to view was a small residential lot in Daytona Beach. On further research, it appeared that lot next door had sold in the $30,000 range. The minimum bid for the lot was about $750, so Laurence decided that we should set a very low bid amount even though we hadn't seen the lot. We thought that if the lot was worth $30,000, we would keep our bid amount below $6,000. We assumed that at this price, someone would outbid us anyway.

When Laurence had finished at the Osceola County auction, he received a phone call from Matt. The conversation went like this:

"Hey Laurence, I just purchased that piece of land in Daytona Beach you researched for $5,800. Are you sure you researched it correctly?...Because it seemed too cheap."

As soon as Laurence heard these words, his heart sank. Laurence rushed back to the office to view the property on the Property Appraiser's website and realized he had made a mistake. Doing research when you are tired can be very detrimental to your investments, as we discovered. Laurence had misread the information on the lot sales in the area, and the neighboring lot which had sold for $30,000 also contained a <u>home</u> on it. Simply put, the HOMES with the land were selling for $30,000, not just the land. Ouch.

We knew we're in this together, so we immediately began thinking of solutions to retrieve our $5,800 investment. We came to the conclusion that if $5000 was the worst mistake we would make in real estate, it wouldn't be the end of the world.

After finding out the potentially bad news, we drove over to Daytona Beach to view the lot. This lot was in a less-than-desirable area of town, and across the street sat several abandoned public houses. We would definitely not have purchased this lot if we had viewed it prior to the sale. The only positive note was that the lot was located very close to 3 local colleges.

Two weeks later, we were sitting in our accountant's office explaining our mistake purchase. He smiled, and informed us that all of the public housing across the street from our lot was due to be demolished and replaced by a $100 million housing and city redevelopment named the "Hope 6 Project". Sure enough, 2 weeks later, a sign appeared across the street announcing the city's redevelopment plans. You can imagine the relief we felt when we saw this sign!

Even though the cash outlay was only $5,800, we hate to make any type of mistake purchases. At the time of writing this book, Hope 6 construction was delayed due to the discovery of an American Bald Eagle nest! The project was placed on hold until the Eagle moved to another location.

We then decided to keep the lot until Hope 6 was completed, at which point we would either sell the lot, or develop it. The land is zoned for multifamily use and can support a triplex easily. We could build triplex for about $225,000. The market value of that triplex after construction would be about $300,000.

We just recently closed on this property 11/01/2006, for a sales price of $36,000. This sale gave us an approximately 500% gross return.

(Transfer Amt $ 5800)
Instrument# 2004-199233

DR-506   **Book: 5378**
Page: 3927

Tax Deed File No. ___7534-97___

Property Identification No. ___5238-27-00-0010___

TAX DEED

State of Florida
County of Volusia

The following Tax Sale Certificate Numbered 7534-97 issued on DECEMBER 8, 2003 was filed in the office of the tax collector of this County and application made for the issuance of a tax deed, the applicant having paid or redeemed all other taxes or tax sale certificates on the land described as required by law to be paid or redeemed, and the costs and expenses of this sale, and due notice of sale having been published as required by law, and no person entitled to do so having appeared to redeem said land; such land was on the ___10TH___ day of ___AUGUST___, ___2004___, offered for sale as required by law for cash to the highest bidder and was sold to ___LONDON MERIDIAN INC___ whose address is _____ ORLANDO FL 32807 _____, being the highest bidder and having paid the sum of their bid as required by the Laws of Florida.

NOW, on this ___10TH___ day of ___AUGUST___, ___2004___, in the County of Volusia, State of Florida, in consideration of the sum of ($ _5,800.00_) FIVE THOUSAND EIGHT HUNDRED AND ___NO/100___ * * Dollars, being the amount paid pursuant to the Laws of Florida does hereby sell the following lands situated in the County and State aforesaid and described as follows:

LOTS 1 & 2 PLEASANT PARK DAYTONA PER MAP BOOK 7 PAGE 79 PER DEATH CERTIFICATE # 6097-01389

Diane M. Matousek,
Clerk of the Circuit Court of Volusia County

By: ___D L Ruegger___
D L RUEGGER, Deputy Clerk
Volusia County, Florida

Witness: ___Pat Matzinger___
PAT MATZINGER
___Lori Diggs___
LORI DIGGS

STATE OF FLORIDA
COUNTY OF VOLUSIA

On this ___10TH___ day of ___AUGUST___, ___2004___, before me ___KAREN CHITTY___ personally appeared D L RUEGGER, Deputy Clerk of the Circuit Court or County Comptroller in and for the State and this County known to me to be the person described in, and who executed the foregoing instrument, and acknowledged the execution of this instrument to be their own free act and deed for the use and purposes therein mentioned.

Witness my hand and official seal date aforesaid.

KAREN J. CHITTY
MY COMMISSION # CC 990847
EXPIRES: Apri. 29, 2005
Bonded Thru Notary Public Underwriters

EXHIBIT K

Golf Anyone?

We are both avid golf enthusiasts, and when we are not in the office making deals or on the road viewing properties, you can usually find us at one of Orlando's many wonderful golf courses, trying to improve our 90s score. Unfortunately for Matt, after scoring 90 on the first 9 holes, it only gets worse on the last nine holes!

As the golf nuts that we are, we were particularly excited about a property listed for upcoming sale in the Polk County auction. Polk County is located between Orlando and Tampa, and is one of the premier retirement areas in the USA. The property was a 4 bedroom, 2 bath, 1940 square foot pool home located in the gated Southern Dunes Golf and County Club in Haines City, FL. We were successful in bidding on this property; we paid $210,800, and since we were prepared to spend up to $240,000, this was a good result.

While we preach never to buy a property sight unseen, we broke our rule on this property. Laurence was in London on business and Matt decided to be lazy and not view the property. There were several reasons we purchased this property sight unseen. It was located in an exclusive golf community where the course was rated 7th best in Florida and 27th best in United States at the time (according to a fellow golfer). Also, due to the recent hurricanes, we expected some property damage; but we bear in mind that damage is always repairable, so this was a calculated risk. The reality is that it could have been a disaster if the property had burned to the ground without Matt's knowledge. After that day, we swore never to buy another property sight unseen.

After the purchase, Matt arrived with a locksmith. Since we believed that no one was living in the house, we gained immediate access to the property. This house looked unlived in, though it was fully furnished. When we contacted the Homeowners Association, we found out that the owner of the property had purchased it 4 years ago as a rental and had never been heard from since. The mail man had been delivering to this address for years, and informed us that the owners lived in the property for 2 months at the beginning, and then were never seen again. The owner, who lived in South America, owed 4 years' worth of Homeowners Association fees ($4628.58), as well as real estate taxes. Most of the time, when a property owner resides overseas, it is more difficult for the county to contact them, so sale notification papers tend to go undelivered.

It appeared as if the house had never been occupied. The furniture looked brand new and the beds had never been slept in. The house needed some minor updating, including removal of the dark green carpets and the replacement of the linoleum floor. We had the outside of the house repainted, installed tile, and we personally landscaped the yard. We repaired the sprinklers, and we hired a local company to maintain the pool in our absence. We advertised the personal possessions in the Public Notices section of the local newspaper, but these items were never claimed.

Most of the properties in this neighborhood were selling for between $150 and $160 a square foot. Because the United States was at war with Iraq, and most of the visitors to this area were from overseas, the rental market had slowed down considerably. This was concerning to us, and even though we knew we had a purchased a great investment with huge long-term growth potential, we wanted to sell. There were quite a few properties listed for sale in the same subdivision, and we discovered that most buyers targeting the area were investors from outside the USA looking for a vacation property. In general, their plans were to live in for a month or two, then rent out the property for the remainder of the year.

At the time, we were working on a deal to purchase 10 condominium units, so we were in need of a LOT of cash—$1.47 million in cash, to be exact. We simply did not have access to this amount of money at the time. We considered partnering with other investors, but even with a formed partnership, we knew we would need to sell this property in order to close on our condos. We had over $220,000 tied up in this property.

We finally accepted an offer of $307,500 from a couple in Massachusetts. However, the title company was delaying closing, so our condo deal came right down to the wire. The day we finally closed on the property in Haines City, we went straight to another title company the <u>same day</u> and closed on the condominium units. In real estate, timing is everything!

Tax Deed File No. **2005-0225**
Property Id: **20-27-27-749027-000430**

TAX DEED

STATE OF FLORIDA, COUNTY OF POLK

The following Tax Sale Certificate Numbered <u>17684</u> issued on 5/31/2002
<u>31st day of May, 2002</u> was filed in the office of the Tax Collector of this County
and applications made for the issuance of a tax deed, the applicant having paid or redeemed
all other taxes or tax sale certificates on the land described as required by law to be
paid or redeemed, and the costs and expenses of this sale, and due notice of sale having
been published as required by law, and no person entitled to do so having appeared to
redeem said land; such land was on the 10th day of March, 2005 offered for sale.

NOW, on this **10th day of March, 2005**, in the County of <u>POLK</u>
State of Florida, in consideration of the sum of ($210,800.00)
<u>Two Hundred Ten Thousand Eight Hundred 00/100</u> Dollars, being the amount
pursuant to the Law of Florida, Polk County, a political subdivision of the state
of Florida, does hereby sell to:

LONDON MERIDIAN INC

whose address is ▮▮▮▮▮▮▮▮▮ ORLANDO FL 32807

The following lands situated in the County and State aforesaid and described as
follows:

SOUTHERN DUNES ESTATES PHASE TWO PB 108 PG 14 LOT 43

INSTR # 2005054045
BK 06115 PG 0588 PG(s)1
RECORDED 03/10/2005 01:33:31 PM
RICHARD M WEISS, CLERK OF COURT
POLK COUNTY
DEED DOC 1,475.60
RECORDING FEES 10.00
RECORDED BY M Petrovich

Section 20, Township 27 South, Range 27 East
INCLUDES 2003 TAXES
Subject to Liens pursuant to 197.552 Florida Statutes

THE SALE OF THE ABOVE DESCRIBED PROPERTY OCCURRED PURSUANT TO CHAPTER 197 OF THE
FLORIDA STATUTES.

Richard M. Weiss
Clerk of the Circuit Court, Polk County, Florida

Witness:

Mary Ann Petrovich
Mary Ann Petrovich

By: _Rochelle E. Rowles_
Rochelle E. Rowles
Drawer CC-8, Post Office Box 9000
Bartow, FL 33831-9000

Tina Reed
Tina Reed

RICHARD M. WEISS, CLERK of COURT
Facsimile Signature as Authorized
STATE OF FLORIDA, COUNTY OF POLK by Florida Statute Section 116.34

On this **10th day of March, 2005** ,before me personally appeared
<u>Rochelle E. Rowles</u> ,Deputy Clerk to **RICHARD M. WEISS** ,Clerk of the Circuit
Court, Polk County, Florida, known to me to be the person described in, and who executed
the foregoing instrument, and acknowledged the execution of this instrument to be of
his/her own free act and deed for the use and purposes therein mentioned.

Witness my hand and official seal date aforesaid.

Prepared by: Mary Ann Petrovich, Deputy Clerk
RICHARD M. WEISS, CLERK CIRCUIT COURT
P O Box 9000, Drawer CC-8
Bartow, Florida 33831

MARY ANN PETROVICH
Notary Public, State of Florida
My comm. expires Oct. 10, 2008
Comm. No. DD 351699

Notary Public

DR-206 R. 10/99

EXHIBIT L-1

OMB Approval No. 2502-0265

A. Settlement Statement	B. Type of Loan

First American Title Insurance Company
Settlement Statement

1-5. Loan Type Conv. Unins.	
6. File Number 2027-837786	
7. Loan Number 111764058	
8. Mortgage Insurance Case Number	

C. Note: This form is furnished to give you a statement of actual settlement costs. Amounts paid to and by the settlement agent are shown. Items marked "(POC)" were paid outside the closing; they are shown here for informational purposes and are not included in the totals.

D. Name of Borrower:
3 Laphan Lane, South Dartmouth, MA 02748

E. Name of Seller: London Meridian Inc.
                    ORLANDO, FL 32807

F. Name of Lender: America's Wholesale Lenders
500 Winderley Place Suite 112
Maitland, FL 32751

G. Property Location: 1697 Waterview Loop, Haines City, FL

H. Settlement Agent: First American Title Insurance Company	I.
Address: 206 West Oak Street, Suite B, Kissimmee, FL 34741	Settlement Date: 09/12/2005
Place of Settlement Address: 206 West Oak Street, Suite B, Kissimmee, FL 34741	Print Date: 09/10/2005, 10:01 AM
	Disbursement Date: 09/14/2005

J. Summary of Borrower's Transaction		K. Summary of Seller's Transaction	
100. Gross Amount Due From Borrower		400. Gross Amount Due To Seller	
101. Contract Sales Price	307,500.00	401. Contract Sales Price	307,500.00
102. Personal Property		402. Personal Property	
103. Settlement charges to borrower (line 1400)	10,003.34	403. Total Deposits	1,000.00
104.		404.	
105.		405.	
Adjustments for items paid by seller in advance		Adjustments for items paid by seller in advance	
106. City/town taxes		406. City/town taxes	
107. County taxes		407. County taxes	
108. Assessments		408. Assessments	
109. Association Dues 09/14/05 to 10/01/05 @$152.00/qtr	28.32	409. Association Dues 09/14/05 to 10/01/05 @$152.00/qtr	28.32
110.		410.	
111.		411.	
112.		412.	
113.		413.	
114.		414.	
115.		415.	
120. Gross Amount Due From Borrower	317,531.66	420. Gross Amount Due To Seller	308,528.32
200. Amounts Paid By Or In Behalf of Borrower		500. Reductions In Amount Due to Seller	
201. Deposit or earnest money	5,000.00	501. Excess deposit (see instructions)	
202. Principal amount of new loan(s)	200,000.00	502. Settlement charges (line 1400)	23,717.50
203. Existing loan(s) taken subject		503. Existing loan(s) taken subject	
204.		504. Payoff of first mortgage loan	
205.		505. Payoff of second mortgage loan	
206.		506. Disbursed as Proceeds ($5000.00)	
207.		507.	
208.		508.	
209.		509.	
Adjustments for items unpaid by seller		Adjustments for items unpaid by seller	
210. City/town taxes		510. City/town taxes	
211. County taxes 01/01/05 to 09/14/05 @$3523.70/yr	2,471.42	511. County taxes 01/01/05 to 09/14/05 @$3523.70/yr	2,471.42
212. Assessments		512. Assessments	
213.		513.	
214.		514.	
215.		515.	
216.		516.	
217.		517.	
218.		518.	
219.		519.	
220. Total Paid By/For Borrower	207,471.42	520. Total Reduction Amount Due Seller	26,188.92
300. Cash At Settlement From/To Borrower		600. Cash At Settlement To/From Seller	
301. Gross amount due from Borrower (line 120)	317,531.66	601. Gross amount due to Seller (line 420)	308,528.32
302. Less amounts paid by/for Borrower (line 220)	207,471.42	602. Less reductions in amounts due to Seller (line 520)	26,188.92
303. Cash (X From) (To) Borrower	110,060.24	603. Cash (X To) (From) Seller	282,339.40

The HUD-1 Settlement Statement which I have prepared is a true and accurate account of this transaction. I have caused or will cause the funds to be disbursed in accordance with this statement.

Settlement Agent: Date:

* See Supplemental

EXHIBIT L-2

EXHIBIT L-3

Daytona Beach Duplex

One of our favorite Tax Deed purchases was a property located in Daytona Beach, FL. At the time of this purchase, Daytona was one of Florida's last places to buy affordable beach-side real estate. Daytona had entered a transitional stage where many developers were building Panama City Beach style high-rise condominiums or converting old hotel buildings into condos (better known as condo conversions).

The duplex we purchased contained two 2 bed, 1 bath, 800 square foot units. The most attractive feature of this duplex was its close proximity to the beach; 3 houses and a road (US-A1A) were all that separated our duplex from the sand.

We purchased this property for $132,000, but we were prepared to go as high as $160,000. We felt this property was worth at least $240,000 in good condition, and properties such as these were very hard to come by.

We decided to meet with a city planning representative to see if the duplex could be expanded. Could we build a second story or an additional residence? Could we convert the rear detached garage into a studio apartment? Unfortunately, the answers to our questions were all no. The city planner informed us that our duplex was considered non-conforming and pre-existing, which means that our duplex was built on land that was no longer zoned for duplex, but was grandfathered in because it was already built. If we were to modify the dimension, square footage, or build another story, we would have to conform to the single family home zoning laws.

Since demolishing the duplex and building an expensive single family home was not financially viable, we chose to leave the property standing and not make any structural changes. That may change in the future as the older surrounding houses are purchased, demolished, and rebuilt.

The duplex was a single-story building sheltered from the wind by other two-story buildings on the street, enabling it to endure 3 hurricanes without damage.

Another reason why this is one of our favorite properties is because we completed most of the renovations ourselves. These renovations included new kitchens, a new screened-in porch, interior and exterior paint, new carpet and tile, new electrical and plumbing, and new landscaping. After 8 weeks of hard work and hundreds of miles of wear and tear on our vehicles, we decided to keep the property as a rental. We knew this was a keeper and a very solid long term investment.

We turned the property over to a rental manager for a standard 10% management fee. Since our homes and offices are located in Orlando, it is nice to sleep well knowing there are qualified people managing our property.

The property was appraised in late 2005 for $315,000. We refinanced the property and took out a loan for $159,000 to repay our upfront costs and most of our rehab costs.

After renting the property for one year, we sold this property in April 2006 for $320,000.

Completing the renovations ourselves gave us a good understanding of evaluating repair costs. This ensured that, in the future, we received fair bids from contractors, because we knew the material costs in relation to specific jobs.

Doc stamps 924.00
(Transfer Amt $ 132000)
Instrument# 2004-228414
DR-506   **Book: 5398**   Tax Deed File No. __9612-01_____
           Page: 2599   Property Identification No. ___5309-28-00-0080_____

TAX DEED

State of Florida
County of Volusia

The following Tax Sale Certificate Numbered __9612-01__ issued on __MAY 28, 2002__ was filed in the office of the tax collector of this County and application made for the issuance of a tax deed, the applicant having paid or redeemed all other taxes or tax sale certificates on the land described as required by law to be paid or redeemed, and the costs and expenses of this sale, and due notice of sale having been published as required by law, and no person entitled to do so having appeared to redeem said land; such land was on the __14TH__ day of __SEPTEMBER__, __2004__, offered for sale as required by law for cash to the highest bidder and was sold to __LONDON MERIDIAN INC__ whose address is ▮▮▮▮▮▮▮▮▮▮▮▮
~~being the highest bidder and having paid the sum of their bid as required by the Laws of Florida~~

NOW, on this __14TH__ day of __SEPTEMBER__, __2004__, in the County of Volusia, State of Florida, in consideration of the sum of ($ __132,000.00__) __ONE HUNDRED THIRTY TWO THOUSAND AND__ __NO/100__ * * Dollars, being the amount paid pursuant to the Laws of Florida does hereby sell the following lands situated in the County and State aforesaid and described as follows:

LOT 8 NELSON & BORIS SUB ATLANTIC CITY

Diane M. Matousek,
Clerk of the Circuit Court of Volusia County

By: ___~~DL Ruegger~~___
D L RUEGGER, Deputy Clerk
Volusia County, Florida

Witness: _____
PAT MATZINGER
_____
LORI DIGGS

STATE OF FLORIDA
COUNTY OF VOLUSIA
On this __14TH__ day of __SEPTEMBER__, __2004__, before me __KAREN CHITTY__ personally appeared __D L RUEGGER,__ __Deputy__ Clerk of the Circuit Court or County Comptroller in and for the State and this County known to me to be the person described in, and who executed the foregoing instrument, and acknowledged the execution of this instrument to be their own free act and deed for the use and purposes therein mentioned.
Witness my hand and official seal date aforesaid.

KAREN J. CHITTY
MY COMMISSION # CC 990847
EXPIRES: April 29, 2005
Bonded Thru Notary Public Underwriters

CL-0009-8412

EXHIBIT M-1

P. 1/2

A. Settlement Statement

U.S. Department of Housing
and Urban Development

OMB No. 2502-0265

B. Type of Loan

1. ☐ FHA	2. ☐ RHS	3. ☒ Conv. Unins.	6. File Number	7. Loan Number	8. Mortgage Insurance Case Number
4. ☐ VA	5. ☐ Conv. Ins.		06-089		

C. Note: This form is furnished to give you a statement of actual settlement costs. Amounts paid to and by the settlement agent are shown. Items marked "(p.o.c.)" were paid outside the closing; they are shown here for information purposes and are not included in the totals.

D. Name and Address of Borrower	E. Name and Address of Seller	F. Name and Address of Lender
███████ 6112 OBERLIN AVE GLEN ECHO, MD 20812	LAURENCE A. SAMUELS MATTHEW MERDIAN ███████	

G. Property Location	H. Settlement Agent
611 LENOX AVENUE DAYTONA BEACH, FL 32118	Harry G. Reid, III - Attorney at Law

	Place of Settlement	I. Settlement Date
	1120 W. First Street, Suite B Sanford, Florida 32771	04/27/06

J. SUMMARY OF BORROWER'S TRANSACTION:		K. SUMMARY OF SELLER'S TRANSACTION:	
100. GROSS AMOUNT DUE FROM BORROWER		400. GROSS AMOUNT DUE TO SELLER	
101. Contract sales price	320,000.00	401. Contract sales price	320,000.00
102. Personal property		402. Personal property	
103. Settlement charges to borrower (line 1400)	255.00	403.	
104.		404.	
105.		405.	
Adjustments for items paid by seller in advance		Adjustments for items paid by seller in advance	
106. City/town taxes	to	406. City/town taxes	to
107. County taxes	to	407. County taxes	to
108. Solid Waste	to	408. Solid Waste	to
109.		409.	
110.		410.	
111.		411.	
112.		412.	
120. GROSS AMOUNT DUE FROM BORROWER	320,255.00	420. GROSS AMOUNT DUE TO SELLER	320,000.00
200. AMOUNTS PAID BY OR IN BEHALF OF BORROWER		500. REDUCTIONS IN AMOUNT TO SELLER	
201. Deposit or earnest money		501. Excess Deposit (see instructions)	
202. Principal amount of new loan(s)		502. Settlement charges to seller (line 1400)	23,596.00
203. Existing loan(s) taken subject to		503. Existing loan(s) taken subject to	
204.		504. Payoff of first mortgage loan	159,757.79
205.		EDGAR BARNETT & JUDITH BARNETT 505. Payoff of second mortgage loan	
206.		506.	
207.		507.	
208.		508.	
209.		509.	
Adjustments for items unpaid by seller		Adjustments for items unpaid by seller	
210. City/town taxes	to	510. City/town taxes	to
211. County taxes	to	511. County taxes	to
212. Solid Waste	to	512. Solid Waste	to
213. TAXES 1/1/06 TO 4/27/06	1,167.44	513. TAXES 1/1/06 TO 4/27/06	1,167.44
214.		514.	
215.		515.	
216.		516.	
217.		517.	
218.		518.	
219.		519.	
220. TOTAL PAID BY / FOR BORROWER	1,167.44	520. TOTAL REDUCTION AMOUNT DUE SELLER	184,515.23
300. CASH AT SETTLEMENT FROM OR TO BORROWER		600. CASH AT SETTLEMENT TO OR FROM SELLER	
301. Gross amount due from borrower (line 120)	320,255.00	601. Gross amount due to seller (line 420)	320,000.00
302. Less amounts paid by/for borrower (line 220)	1,167.44	602. Less reduction amount due to seller (line 520)	184,515.23
303. CASH FROM BORROWER	319,087.56	603. CASH TO SELLER	135,484.77

EXHIBIT M-2

Land Ahoy! 1000% Treasure! Or A Diamond in the Rough

We saved our most lucrative Tax Deed investment for last. We share this story not for bragging purposes, but rather to show you a real life example of the possibilities within the Tax Deed investment market.

Orlando's real estate prices have risen sharply between 2003 and 2006, causing some people look elsewhere to purchase affordable homes. Sanford is one of the up-and-coming areas to live in central Florida due to its affordable prices and convenient location. Many decades ago, Sanford used to be the hub of central Florida. People would journey to Orlando by boat, as there were no viable roadways. Since then, times have changed, and Orlando has become the hub of social and residential activity.

In June 2004, we bid on 8.8 acres of land in Sanford. We purchased this tract of land for $34,000, which seemed very reasonable at the time. The land was cheap because it contained several problems that needed to be resolved. This land had never been touched, and was overgrown with brush, vines, and trees. One of the biggest problems was that only 2.25 acres was usable; the rest was deemed wetlands. The Future Land Use of the entire property was Conservation Area, but the zoning was R-3, indicating multi-family use. We knew that these problems could be fixed, but they would take time. Dealing with the city on issues like these can be difficult, and due to our inexperience, this took us much longer than it would have taken an experienced developer.

Three days after purchasing the land, we received a call from a person offering to sell us another 4.04 acres of land in Sanford for $17,000. His property was located behind ours but was inaccessible, so he wanted to sell it as quickly as possible. We believe he purchased it without viewing and researching it first—another reason why you should never buy sight unseen! Even though his property was also designated as wetlands, it contained one acre of high and dry land zoned for Commercial use. We also knew that the additional wetland areas could be sold for $5,000 to $10,000 per acre.

We were able to purchase a total of 12.85 acres of land for $52,000. Next door to our property was a large church, who we contacted to see if they might be interested in purchasing our land. At first they declined our offer. However, 6 months later, they contacted us to ask if the land was still for sale. The church explained that they wanted to expand their congregation size but did not have enough parking spaces to facilitate an expansion. They explained that our land would be used to provide additional parking spaces. The church offered us $390,000 for the land. By this time, however, we had completed engineering plans for a 14 unit town home development, so we decided to decline the church's offer.

During the planning stage for the London Meridian Preserve development, we received an offer for the land. We were quite reluctant to sell, as we were close to proceeding forward with our first construction project. After some negotiation and a lot of persuasion, we accepted a selling price of $460,000 with a $100,000 down payment. We agreed to hold the $360,000 note at 12% interest for 1 year, which equates to $3600 per month in positive cash flow until the property is refinanced or closed upon. These numbers show quite a return on our original investment; a return of almost 1000%!

We closed on this property on 03/30/2007. The new owner plans to move forward with developing the property according to our original plans.

MARYANNE MORSE, CLERK OF CIRCUIT COURT
SEMINOLE COUNTY
BK 05337 PG 0888
CLERK'S # 2004088700
RECORDED 06/07/2004 03:12:48 PM
DEED DOC TAX 238.00
RECORDING FEES 10.00
RECORDED BY G Harford

Tax Deed File No. _____ 1454-1999 _____
Property
Identification No. _____ 01-20-30-300-0130-0000 _____

DR-506
R. 01/95

Tax Deed

State of Florida

County of _____ Seminole _____

FOR OFFICIAL USE ONLY

The following Tax Sale Certificate Numbered _____ 1454 _____ issued on
_____ May 26, 1999 _____ was filed in the office of the tax collector of this County and application made for
the issuance of a tax deed, the applicant having paid or redeemed all other taxes or tax sale certificates on the land
described as required by law to be paid or redeemed, and the costs and expenses of this sale, and due notice of sale
having been published as required by law, and no person entitled to do so having appeared to redeem said land; such land
was on _____ June 7 _____ , _____ 2004 _____ , offered for sale as required by law for cash to the
highest bidder and was sold to London Meridian Inc

whose address is ▮▮▮▮▮▮▮▮▮▮▮▮▮▮▮▮▮▮▮▮▮▮▮▮ ,being the
highest bidder and having paid the sum of his bid as required by the Laws of Florida.
Now, on this _____ 7th _____ day of _____ June _____ 2004
in the County of _____ Seminole _____ State of Florida, in consideration of the sum
of ($ 34,000.00) Thirty-Four Thousand and 00/100---Dollars,
being the amount paid pursuant to the Laws of Florida does hereby sell the following lands, including any building or other
buildings, fixtures and improvements of any kind and description, situated in the County and State aforesaid and described
as follows: SEC 01 TWP 20S RGE 30E LOT 2 (LESS E 653.05 FT & W 537.8 FT OF E 1190.85 FT OF S 405 FT & NLY
1942.3 FT & RD R/W)

Witness: _____

GERALDINE HARFORD

DEBORAH M. BROWN

_____ (Seal)
Clerk of Circuit Court or County Comptroller
LUANNE WOODLEY FOR MARYANNE MORSE
_____ Seminole _____ County, Florida

State of Florida

County of _____ Seminole _____

On this _____ 7th _____ day of _____ JUNE _____ 2004 before
me _____ HAYDEE ORTIZ _____ personally appeared _____ LUANNE WOODLEY _____
Clerk of the Circuit Court or County Comptroller in and for the State and this County known to me to be the person
described in, and who executed the foregoing instrument, and acknowledged the execution of this instrument to be his own
free act and deed for the use and purposes therein mentioned.

Witness my hand and office seal date aforesaid.

HAYDEE ORTIZ

_____
Deputy Clerk

EXHIBIT N

Prepared by Maryanne Morse, Clerk of the Circuit Court

A. Settlement Statement

U.S. Department of Housing
and Urban Development

OMB No. 2502-0265

B. Type of Loan

1.☐ FHA 2.☐ RHS 3.☒ Conv. Unins.	6. File Number	7. Loan Number	8. Mortgage Insurance Case Number
4.☐ VA 5.☐ Conv. Ins.	07-018		

C. Note: This form is furnished to give you a statement of actual settlement costs. Amounts paid to and by the settlement agent are shown. Items marked "(p.o.c.)" were paid outside the closing; they are shown here for information purposes and are not included in the totals.

D. Name and Address of Borrower	E. Name and Address of Seller	F. Name and Address of Lender
▮▮▮▮▮▮ ORLANDO, FL 32801	LONDON MERIDIAN INTERNATIONAL, LLC ▮▮▮▮ ORLANDO, FL 32801	

G. Property Location	H. Settlement Agent
XXX WOODLAND DR SANFORD, FL 32771	Harry G. Reid, III - Attorney at Law

	Place of Settlement 1120 W. First Street, Suite B Sanford, Florida 32771	I. Settlement Date 03/30/07

J. SUMMARY OF BORROWER'S TRANSACTION:		K. SUMMARY OF SELLER'S TRANSACTION:	
100. GROSS AMOUNT DUE FROM BORROWER		**400. GROSS AMOUNT DUE TO SELLER**	
101. Contract sales price	460,000.00	401. Contract sales price	460,000.00
102. Personal property		402. Personal property	
103. Settlement charges to borrower (line 1400)	255.00	403.	
104.		404.	
105.		405.	
Adjustments for items paid by seller in advance		Adjustments for items paid by seller in advance	
106. City/town taxes to		406. City/town taxes to	
107. County taxes to		407. County taxes to	
108. Solid Waste to		408. Solid Waste to	
109.		409.	
110.		410.	
111.		411.	
112.		412.	
120. GROSS AMOUNT DUE FROM BORROWER	460,255.00	**420. GROSS AMOUNT DUE TO SELLER**	460,000.00
200. AMOUNTS PAID BY OR IN BEHALF OF BORROWER		**500. REDUCTIONS IN AMOUNT DUE TO SELLER**	
201. Deposit or earnest money	100,000.00	501. Excess Deposit (see instructions)	100,000.00
202. Principal amount of new loan(s)		502. Settlement charges to seller (line 1400)	6,110.00
203. Existing loan(s) taken subject to		503. Existing loan(s) taken subject to	
204.		504. Payoff of first mortgage loan	
205.		505. Payoff of second mortgage loan	
206.		506.	
207.		507.	
208.		508.	
209.		509.	
Adjustments for items unpaid by seller		Adjustments for items unpaid by seller	
210. City/town taxes to		510. City/town taxes to	
211. County taxes to		511. County taxes to	
212. Solid Waste to		512. Solid Waste to	
213. No tax prorations per lease agreement		513. No tax prorations per lease agreement	
214.		514.	
215.		515.	
216.		516.	
217.		517.	
218.		518.	
219.		519.	
220. TOTAL PAID BY / FOR BORROWER	100,000.00	**520. TOTAL REDUCTION AMOUNT DUE SELLER**	106,110.00
300. CASH AT SETTLEMENT FROM OR TO BORROWER		**600. CASH AT SETTLEMENT TO OR FROM SELLER**	
301. Gross amount due from borrower (line 120)	460,255.00	601. Gross amount due to seller (line 420)	460,000.00
302. Less amounts paid by/for borrower (line 220)	100,000.00	602. Less reduction amount due to seller (line 520)	106,110.00
303. CASH FROM BORROWER	360,255.00	**603. CASH TO SELLER**	353,890.00

EXHIBIT N

We hope you enjoyed our actual stories. We selected these stories to illustrate the principles we discussed in this book. We did not include these stories to brag. We merely want to provide you with real life examples to motivate and inspire you. We want you to know that anyone can become a Tax Deed real estate investor, and everyone has the possibility of making millions of dollars doing so. We are no geniuses! As our families tell us all the time, "if you guys can do it, anyone can do it".

Q and A with a Tax Deed Official

Recently, we tried to get a Florida Tax Deed Official to answer some questions for this book, so we could provide you with an inside prospective on the Tax Deed process. Unfortunately, government employees were not able to answer our questions due to liability concerns.

We were able to call a very reliable source at one of the Tax Deed offices anonymously, and we got the following answers to our questions. Due to liability issues, we cannot disclose which county we called or who we spoke to. For the purpose of the book, it is not important. Here are the questions we asked and answers we received.

What are the 3 most common questions new investors ask you?

1. Are these properties free and clear of all liens?
2. Can I really buy a house for just the amount of the tax owed?
3. How much do the properties usually sell for?

What are the most common misconceptions or assumptions regarding Tax Deeds?

People believe these properties are free and clear, when sometimes there are liens to be taken care of.

The county does not provide pictures of the properties, nor do we hold keys to any buildings that may be located on a property.

What do you view as the largest obstacle these new investors have to overcome?

Laziness is the largest obstacle. There is a lot of research that is involved with Tax Deed properties, and most people do not want to take the time and effort to complete this research.

What is the most bizarre situation you have seen?

In a different county, I heard of a gentleman who purchased property around a lake, and proceed to erect a huge flamingo pink fence that obstructed everyone's lake views. The man then approached each of the residents, demanding they pay him to remove the fence so they could have their lake views back.

How has the Tax Deed process changed over the years?

Different aspects of the laws change periodically. Most recently, the law changed so that the applicant on a particular certificate cannot opt to put the property on the "List of Lands Available". If no one bids on the property, it is automatically struck back to the applicant.

What common element do you find that investors have?

The most common elements are greed, determination, and intelligence. I don't mean greed in a derogatory way, but in a 'desire to achieve' way.

What would you say is the most difficult part of the research involved?

The hardest part is navigating the Comptroller's website for both Tax Deed and owner information. Also, navigating the Property Appraiser's website to obtain property information can be difficult.

What is the most common reason people have not paid their real estate taxes?

People usually fall upon hard times, which is why they become late on their taxes. Other people move and do not notify the Property Appraiser's office of their address change, and therefore do not receive their tax bill, so they forget to pay.

If you could offer one piece of free advice to new investors, what would it be?

Do your research!!

Final Words

Deals like the ones we have written about here do exist in the Tax Deed world. They are not a dime a dozen, but they do exist, and we are living proof of that. If you work hard, complete your research, and take the time to perform your due diligence, we know you will find many successful deals just like the ones we found.

We don't believe in get quick rich schemes. Remember the saying,

If it sounds too good to be true, it probably is.

This is true 90% of the time. The other 10%, great deals are right under your nose. There is some amount of luck and timing involved, as not everything is calculated.

You may attend auctions where first-time bidders pay too much for properties because they are inexperienced in evaluating the market prices. This happens all the time. You may attend 50 auctions and come away empty-handed every time. Do not get discouraged. Remember the classic 100-10-1 real estate rule. For every 100 properties you look at, 10 will be of interest and only 1 will be purchased. Those are standard numbers to go by. You have to be mentally prepared for this, especially in today's competitive real estate market. However, there may be times where you will attend 3 auctions in 3 weeks and purchase 3 properties, all at great prices. Maybe the people who usually bid are away on vacation, or maybe they do not have the available capital and are taking some time away from the auctions until they sell their inventory.

All these scenarios exist, and you must expect them. Sometimes people are simply willing to pay more for a home because they want to repair it while they live in it, or maybe they see values that you don't. There have been many times when we have thought about increasing our bid amounts by a few thousand dollars.

Sometimes at these auctions, you can get bitten by bidder's fever. The adrenaline you feel at the auction is exhilarating and your brain is telling you to bid more. Don't get caught up in this frenzy. We urge you to sit back, calculate a price, and stick to it. There are many deals around the corner, and even if you didn't get the property you had your heart set on, there will be a better deal around the corner.

Remember that patience is a virtue and good things come to those who wait!

Helpful Websites

www.taxdeedbook.com
www.google.com
www.maps.com
www.zillow.com
www.mapquest.com
www.ebay.com
www.propsourcebook.com
www.loopnet.com
www.bbb.org
www.suntrustmortgage.com/ecotter

Disclaimer:

There are many risks associated with investing in real estate, or any investment, for that matter. Always consult a lawyer, attorney, or certified planning advisor before making any investment. London Meridian International LLC / London Meridian Publishing LLC, its agents, publishers, or employees shall not be held liable to anyone for any errors, omissions, or inaccuracies under any circumstances. When we reference monetary gains, it may refer to gains in net worth or gains through sales resulting in profits. The entire risk for utilizing the information contained in this book rests solely on the users of this book. This book does not make any specific investment recommendations. Any recommendations listed in this book are for informational purposes only. Extensive research of any investment property will exceed the information found in this book or any extension of this literature. All information in this book was deemed true and accurate at the time of writing. We are not advising you to make any investment; we are merely providing you with great information so you can make an informed decision.

Made in the USA
Lexington, KY
28 January 2014